Dance to Your Own Tune

Dance to Your Own Tune

Go Within and Change Your Life

Bernadette Reynolds

BALBOA.
PRESS

A DIVISION OF HAY HOUSE

Balboa Press books may be ordered through booksellers or by contacting:

Balboa Press
A Division of Hay House
1663 Liberty Drive
Bloomington, IN 47403
www.balboapress.com.au
1 (877) 407-4847

Because of the dynamic nature of the Internet, any web addresses or links contained in this book may have changed since publication and may no longer be valid. The views expressed in this work are solely those of the author and do not necessarily reflect the views of the publisher, and the publisher hereby disclaims any responsibility for them.

The author of this book does not dispense medical advice or prescribe the use of any technique as a form of treatment for physical, emotional, or medical problems without the advice of a physician, either directly or indirectly. The intent of the author is only to offer information of a general nature to help you in your quest for emotional and spiritual well-being. In the event you use any of the information in this book for yourself, which is your constitutional right, the author and the publisher assume no responsibility for your actions.

Any people depicted in stock imagery provided by Thinkstock are models, and such images are being used for illustrative purposes only.
Certain stock imagery © Thinkstock.

Printed in the United States of America.

ISBN: 978-1-4525-2486-3 (sc)
ISBN: 978-1-4525-2487-0 (e)

Balboa Press rev. date: 07/30/2014

STORY CONTENT

INTRODUCTON

The book you are about to read is about my life. I am the eldest of eleven children so I have seen and experienced many highs and lows. There is twenty years difference between my youngest sister and myself. Due to my mother needing support with the younger children I took on the role of helper. I was obviously proficient in this role because my younger siblings saw me as much a mother as they did a sister.

In amongst all of this I was growing physically but not emotionally. When I was eleven years old my parents had a photo taken of me with my brothers and sisters. People who saw the photo thought I was the mother due to my physical appearance, but emotionally I would be playing catch up for many years.

Secondary school was a very rough ride as I was bullied because I did not fit in. I had no idea of who I was so I had no confidence or self esteem. My only respite was when I was in my second year and I had a lovely English teacher who encouraged me in my writing. From then on I would continuously write stories at home then take them to class to show her. No matter how bad they were she supported me in what I was doing because she realised it was the only way I could express my unexpressed feelings.

I was married to my first husband at twenty. Emotionally I was still a child struggling in an adult world.

After having my two daughters it was time for me to identify myself as a mature person. My husband was a wonderful person who supported me through tantrums and dummy spits. Eventually it all became too much for us both so we chose to go our separate ways.

During this time I found addictions to help create the person who I aspired to be. First I had to be slim to fit in so I became a gym and aerobics junkie, then running became my friend. I then walked the path of first anorexia followed by bulimia which controlled me for many years. During this time I still needed confidence so I discovered alcohol and with the bulimia this became my way of life.

Somewhere amongst this I met my now husband Howard who has been my rock. I felt as though I had come home to a place of safety and security. Howard knew I still had a lot of maturing to do and was prepared to stand by me while I did it. He took on the role of step father to my daughters with responsibility and a fountain of love he readily shared with them.

He showed me how I could fill every need I would ever have. He was caring, understanding and supportive of my daughters through their teenage years whereas I was still grappling with my emotional self. Alcohol seemed to fill every gap for me but in the process it created even more. Eventually everything became too overwhelming so I decided it was time for me to leave the pain of living behind.

There was no continuity in my life so there is no continuity to this book. I have been writing my stories for twelve years and looking back over them I can see threads coming together to create a whole me. During this time I gave up alcohol only to return to the same because my intent was not backed up with commitment.

For twelve months I have been addiction free and this includes caffeine. I now know the meaning of freedom, health, vitality and the love of a family who now have a wife, mother and grandmother who is present every moment of every day.

DANCE TO YOUR OWN TUNE!

We are on earth to dance to our own tune!
We have to know who *I* the individual is.
Do we take on other people's words to be our words?
Do we choose to live a life fraught with doom and gloom?
Conversely do we choose the path of freedom?
We inadvertently have to know freedom within ourselves
before we can possibly live a life as a free spirit!
We may choose to dance behind the mask of a clown.
or, we may choose to dance the dance of exposure
through our truth in thoughts, words and actions.
We can dance with the gentleness of a summer's breeze.
or, the frenzy of a tornado tearing, ripping and pulling
everything to us then leaving us in its destructive wake.
Nothing matters when we are dancing to our own tune
as it is about me learning about me.
If I do not know me how can I expect anyone else to?
If I can't have a relationship with me how can I possibly
have a relationship with another?
Allow your steps to breathe life into the places within that
are suffocating through denial and neglect.
Dance into your pain and despair to release any fears holding
you in a place where you do not want to be.
Dance into and around every negative in your life then allow
your torch to shine on these negatives to bring positive outcomes.
You must hold onto the awareness to *never stop dancing*.
If you stop you will find yourself stuck and your flexibility waning.
Your light will then move further, then further away from you.
You may dance around other people's advice and understanding
but you must *never* dance to their tune.
Dance your dance with steps so light you will leave
no tell tale signs for anyone to follow.
We are on earth at this time to **DANCE TO
OUR OWN TUNE** and no one else's!

LET GO, SAYS MR WALLABY

Let go of what? Mr Wallaby.
Let go of the illusions you have manifested as your reality then given permission to fuel your perception of life.

Your inner paddocks have created your outer paddocks. You fenced yourselves in then hid your key after your gate was locked.

It mystifies us wallabies as to why you have done this. The aborigines had the greatest respect for this magnificent land. They called every creature great and small their neighbour and killed when they were hungry. We lived a great many years in this manner and it served the purpose of us all.

Then more humans appeared and showed us no respect by trampling over and desecrating this virgin land. Many had their lives terminated by these humans who carried weapons of destruction. *FOR WHAT*?

There was balance and harmony before you arrived in your boats. Bloodshed, death and destruction followed your every footstep.

We look at you humans and feel extremely perplexed because what you are looking for you already have. Your problem is you look to other people and places to find what is inside of you. It is now time to pull out your key then unlock the gate and free yourself.

We know safety comes from within but when this is not your truth you manifest insecurities from your fears. This is when the egos penchant for power and control becomes your *Illusion of Reality*.

You then become weaker and weaker because your energy goes into creating a facade you call yourself. Break free of your delusion and carefully created façade to know what is real. Then your energy can be used to manifest the beautiful person you will know as yourself.

In my world I am locked into nothing as my needs are basic. Accordingly I protect my friends and family as we respect rather than destroy. I have my predators and this is in my understanding but over the years more predators have become more apparent. Largely they are humans with guns and humans in vehicles distributing poisons polluting our waterways and our land. We have had to learn to adapt to enable us to survive.

You humans seem to be on a path of destruction or in the larger picture self destruction. It is time to wake up and stop destroying everything belonging to us all so we can all live together in peace and harmony. You humans have to make your choice because we already have made ours. You have to know the only limitations you have are the limitations you have created for yourselves. *Do not let it be too late before you Release to know FREEDOM.*
WAKE UP BEFORE IT IS TOO LATE

THE OWL AND THE DEER

THE MESSAGE

WALK STRONG AND TALL
HOLD YOUR HEAD HIGH
BUT ONLY WITH THE WISDOM OF THE OWL
BE FLEET OF FOOT LIKE THE DEER
KNOW WHEN TO CAMOUFLAGE
THEN WHEN TO MOVE
ONLY WHEN YOU SET YOURSELF FREE
CAN YOU SHOW OTHERS THIS CAN BE DONE
NEVER HOLD THE REINS
AS THIS IS A LOSS OF IDENTITY OF ONE'S SELF
SIT THE WAY THE OWL DOES ON THE DEER
NEVER STOP FEELING THE EARTH
MOVE UNDER YOUR FEET OR
THE WIND IN YOUR HAIR!

A MESSAGE FROM A WISE OLD FLOWER!

Look above then look below
But please do not forget to look at *now*
Because there resides the gifts for all your today's
Now look ahead and take note because,
the gifts you now hold are creating
your today's gifts for tomorrow!

A PERFECT MOTHER

Our earth has many grids
Our earth's grids parallel our grids within
When the earth cries, I cry!
When the earth rejoices, I rejoice!
When the earth nurtures, I nurture!
When the earth feels pain, I feel pain!
I can see the patterns
All earth's grids (meridians) are solid within me
Our Earth Mother's key phrase is – *I DO!*
Our Earth Mother's spirit is – *I AM!*
Our *Perfect Mother* is *Unconditional Love!*

MY PREDATOR AND PREY

MY PREDATOR AND PREY ARE ASPECTS OF MYSELF THAT HAD MY LIFE IN TURMOIL!

I say this with clarity because I spent many years in no man's land before I chose to tame the predator then integrate it with the prey. I realised these two destructive influences tearing my life apart were mine, for me to tame. I had to acknowledge them as an aspect of myself before I could untangle the web I had allowed them to weave.

MY BEGINNINGS

My mother was an only child until the age of fifteen when she was presented with a baby brother. She and her mother spent a great deal of time alone together due to her father going to war. My mother had a very lonely childhood and missed the companionship of brothers and sisters. She had a love of babies so was determined to have many of her own.

MY ARRIVAL

My mother met my father and then married. My mother (an impatient Aries) wanted a child immediately and my father (a conservative Leo) wanted to wait. Nonetheless ten months later I (a sensitive Pisces) arrived to take up residence with them. My parents were thrilled with me but somehow I don't quite believe I felt the same. I think I had fairly high expectations around how my life would be. I obviously disregarded the lessons I had come here to learn.

By the time I was two months old I must have had some inkling because I began to cry for what seemed to my parents like hours in the very early morning. Eventually my parents (for their sanity) would take me in my bassinet into the kitchen and firmly shut the door. This became our routine until I was six months old. I obviously realised at a young age my life on earth was not going to be as exciting as I had envisaged.

CHOICES

Somewhere along the line my predator and prey began their games within me. Eventually I came to recognise each was vying for supremacy to control and manipulate. As I grew older I chose to take on the prey (victim) persona rather than my intimidating predator self. I had to create my niche in life and self responsibility was not on my personal agenda. I could hide aspects of myself I did not want to deal with as the spotlight was not on me.

My mother and father were very religious so I learned from an early age fear preceded love.

I learned to fear a great many things so this encouraged me to go deep within to hide any parts I did not want exposed. I created my own personal belief system from what I now know as an illusion *but* at the time it was very real. I was never encouraged to accept myself as an individual with individual thoughts and beliefs. When unleashed my predator and prey would take me to the highest of highs and then the lowest of lows to leave me in total confusion. It would be years before I could identify myself as an individual with a purpose. Yes, there were always choices but when fear ruled my life I made some very poor ones.

WHO WAS THE BULLY?

The life we live only takes on what we are so I took on the role of a victim; subsequently I brought predators into my life. To do this I kept playing the same game to come up with the same scenario. This always lead me down the path to self-doubt then confusion. I almost welcomed bullies into my life as this reinforced my belief of being a victim.

SABOTAGE?

My mother from time to time gave me a piece of jewellery or other family trinkets to look after. My prey thought this was a wonderful opportunity for me to love and cherish them *but* then my predator would chirp in with, *"you don't deserve this so you will misplace or lose it never to be found again."* Guess what that's exactly what happened. I was devastated and wondered why everything I touched would disappear.

No matter what I did or attempted to do in any aspect of my life the same scenario would play itself out. At the time I felt compelled to blame others or situations for what I eventually realised were my own indiscretions and inadequacies. It never seemed to matter which way I turned there was always the inevitable *brick wall*.

This tug-o-war went on inside of me for many years. I had the ability to sabotage a positive and turn it into a negative very quickly. My ego took over on many occasions to hurt anyone offering me their hand in friendship. My predator would have his sword at the ready to cut down my prey whenever it started to feel the tiniest bit confident.

MY SOLICE?

My greatest pleasure was my beloved bed at night. Once there I could transport myself to places where the predator and prey did not exist. I could curl up and be at peace where no one could see or touch me. Nights were special because my combatants could take off their armour and be as one. This peaceful space was for energising and rejuvenating not fighting and bickering. Then as night turned to day the battle would begin to rage inside of me again.

MORE CHOICES?

As time moved on and my battles within still raged I knew it was time for me to get smart. I decided the best way I could achieve this was to separate my predator from my prey. I put my predator in a cage and threw away the key (or so I thought) and played the victim like a finely tuned violin.

Gradually the predator released itself from its cage and pounced at a time when I was smug in my believing I was in control. I had hold of the reins and I was not going to let them go *but* what a fool I was. The predator found it easy to influence my life as I was plagued by confusion and low self esteem. I was a boat without a rudder in the sea of my own life.

A LOSING BATTLE?

In this state of confusion I took to alcohol like a fish to water. I allowed the predator and prey to play out any game they chose. I really didn't care (or so I said) but in reality I did because I wanted to hide all the parts of myself that did not stand on their own. For many years my predator played its game behind closed doors and my prey would come to the fore in public. Only my immediate family experienced both parts of me and it was not pleasant for any of them.

WHY IS THE BAND PLAYING THE DEATH MARCH?

This battle took place over many years. I was in the middle of a very intense struggle when I heard the death march playing. I looked around to see who else it could have been for *but* I was the only player on my own battlefield. I then knew I had pushed my boundaries as far as they could go so I had to make a choice. At that time death was appealing but somewhere inside I knew this had to be a beginning not an end. It was time for me to put away my armour and call a truce so I could bring the fractured fragments of what I could loosely say was my life together.

WHERE WERE MY STRENGTHS HIDING?

I had to find then learn by delving into the aspects of myself I had kept hidden. I had to bring out my strengths and learn to trust myself and know who I was and why I was here. I had to learn to like then love the person who was waiting patiently to enter into my life. The me that wanted to laugh and have fun, the me that wanted to feel then give and receive love. It was always there but I was too busy feeling sorry for myself to know.

This was the beginning of a very painful recovery. I had to learn to trust myself and walk with my decisions and not fob them off. My quest was to know and love myself from truth and not deceit.

THE LONG AND LONELY JOURNEY TO MYSELF

The road was narrow, rough and pot-holed. I slipped and fell on many occasions but I knew I was the only one responsible for picking myself up and moving forward. In doing this I brought the predator and prey together to be at peace. It has taken years before I had any real inkling of me. My biggest and hardest lesson from this was the realisation that actions do speak louder than words.

I

ACCEPTANCE

THE PREDATOR ACCEPTS NO BOUNDARIES
THE PREY CREATES BOUNDARIES
WITHIN BOUNDARIES
THE TRUTH IS SOMEWHERE IN BETWEEN
WHEN YOU FIND YOUR TRUTH YOU WILL KNOW!

I AM ONE WITH THE EARTH

My heart beats in unison with the spirit of the earth.
My heart beats in unison with the earth's heartbeat.
My footsteps meld with those of the earth.
My breath reverberates then joins with the earth's breath.
My blood flows as it emulates the waterways of the earth.
My lungs take in air that has been cleansed by the plants of the earth.
My hands caress and nurture as a gentle breeze does to the earth.
My ears hear the songs of the earth when the pain
of loneliness threatens to crush my being.
My eyes see beauty where there are no words to describe.
My senses sing and dance with the whisperings of the wind.
My heart feels pain when unguarded words are spoken.
My footsteps become heavy when I am in a state of anger.
My footsteps become light when I am in my place of delight.
My journey is my reality due to this wonderful earth.

SO

Why is it my intent to destroy me?
Why will I not budge when holding a grudge?
Why are my eyes open when I will not see?
Why am I alert to the sounds of pain and not love?
Why do my words come back to haunt me?
Why is my breath harsh and raspy not gentle and loving?
Why does my heart keep searching for love?
Why do I allow my footsteps to become heavy because of anger?
Why do I lose sight of my place of delight?
Why do I allow loneliness to crush my being?
Why do I purge all that is good?
Why do I obey the call of destruction?
Am I one with the earth?
Is this how she feels in her moments of despair?
The difference between her and me is that she absorbs my pain, anger,
misery and I absorb her love, nurturing, beauty and freedom.
It would seem it is time for me to learn to give and
receive rather than take, then take some more.

FEMININE AND MASCULINE

It is imperative for us to grow as an individual to bring our feminine and masculine together for balance and wholeness. This enables us to live our life in peace and harmony. Our steps will be light and purposeful without any quibbling between the feminine and masculine. Unless we can bring these aspects of ourselves together we will always be out of balance as will be evident in our relationships.

THE BATTLEGROUND WITHIN?

My feminine and masculine have had some ding dong battles that tore at the very fibre of my being. It took me a long time to understand what was happening and the importance of bringing them together for my sanity. I believed I was feminine because I am a female but in reality the joke was certainly on me because I could not have been more wrong. My feminine was insecure and vindictive and my masculine was a sheep in wolf's clothing. The masculine thought he was honest and above it all. He certainly had a lot to learn, as a matter of fact the two separate aspects of myself did. I would never have found balance in any area of my life until they both contributed equally for me to be whole.

IS FREEDOM INTANGIBLE?

My feminine wanted freedom. Due to her limited experience of life she had no real understanding what it was she was looking for. She believed if she removed herself from her uneventful life, freedom would be her reward. In doing so she deemed herself incapable of finding the freedom she craved. She had to stop grabbing from other people things she presumed should have been hers. Freedom is an intangible so she could not touch, see or hear it on the physical level because it is a feeling an inner knowing.

ARE YOU A CREATURE OF HABIT?

My life is not any different to his, hers or theirs because we are all creatures of habit. Whether we acknowledge this or not we keep creating routines for ourselves. In and of itself there is no problem with this but we have to be flexible. Unless we are flexible we give ourselves nowhere to move. We will find ourselves stuck and constantly marching up and down on the spot.

I COULD SEE BUT I NEVER SAW

I have spent many hours in nature with my tormented feminine. Somehow she never truly appreciated these experiences because there had to be more. I would immerse myself in the unique beauty of the ocean, mountains or bushlands but my feminine was never satisfied. She would look around her and say "*what's next there has to be more*".

WHO WOULD SABOTAGE FREEDOM?

My feminine had no awareness of beauty in anyone or anything so could never experience freedom. She sabotaged many an occasion with her sulking and selfishness. She never acknowledged another person for trying to help her; in fact she did the opposite and made them pay for any generosity they showed her. She had expectations so as long as she didn't have to contribute to them she could throw the blame onto someone else.

She obviously had delusions of royalty because she expected other people to shower her with gifts she perceived was missing from her life. Her presumption was that if she manipulated and coerced enough people, all the missing pieces of herself would be handed to her on a silver platter. Hers and my relationship was fraught with barriers and obstacles because we existed in a space where illusion and delusion was our reality.

When she was vulnerable she would sulk and hide behind her inner child to play the part of a little girl. She knew it was permissible for little girls to play games and not be made accountable for their behaviour. Her physical may have been mature but her emotional was residing in the past. She was lost in the wilderness of herself so her emotional growth was waiting to be uncaged.

PLEASE RESCUE ME?

I found it easy to be responsible for other people on the pretext they needed me and whatever help I could give them. My feminine found herself sitting in many crevices and wondering why no one was trying to pull her out. She believed she was a rescuer of other people but in this belief she lost sight of the fact the only person who could rescue her was herself.

Typical for a poor me/victim. Remember all the things I have done for you and the help I have given you! So why did I continue walking this path if I was giving so much then receiving so little in return? It seems to me now that I kept digging myself deeper and deeper into my poor me. I held tightly onto a perception of what I thought I was. This was even more pronounced when I felt my life crumbling around me with every vestige exposed for all to see. Many fears attached themselves to the word change when I had to confront myself and heal the damage I caused. It was time for me to make friends with truth and honesty.

WHO'S HOLDING ONTO MY EMOTIONS?

Due to being the eldest of eleven children I knew what responsibility meant. I took on the responsibility of helping my mother and my siblings with ease as my nurturing instincts were very strong. Somewhere along the line I became confused when my feminine craved attention. I was giving her little because I could not bring any semblance of balance into my life.

At times the weight of my responsibilities took their toll because I was blazing a path for my six younger sisters. My mother would say that whatever I did would reflect on the decisions she would make relating to my sisters. For me it was more responsibility to carry around in my kit bag.

SUBTERFUGE OR FANTASY?

I would quite often fantasise about having someone to hold me so I could feel loved and cared for. It took me a long time to know that unless I loved and cared for myself no one else could or would fill my void.

COWARDLY MASCULINE

My masculine was a coward. While pretending to be strong he would lash out and hurt people then go into hiding. He believed in his masculinity and the image he projected was of the utmost importance to him. He would say and do cruel things for a reaction then when he got one he would hide behind the feminine. He knew she would be blamed, and then forgiven, due to her little girl innocence. The feminine found herself apologising and covering up for his indiscretions on many occasions which in reality were feeding his ego.

He was never perturbed at how much trouble the feminine found herself in. She knew of his cowardice so would come to his rescue and smooth things over whenever possible. She took on his insecurities as her insecurities because she lacked the courage to face and confront him.

He lacked courage and would not make decisions so would pass the responsibility onto the feminine to deal with. In his finite wisdom he would set about sabotaging her decisions by proving to her how pathetic she was. Due to him being incarcerated in his misguided sense of superiority he would take great satisfaction in degrading her by saying she got it wrong again. "See she can't get anything right because the fool that she is, she stuffs it up every time."

BATTLE OF THE OPPOSING TRIBES

Eventually the feminine had had enough. She was sick of being abused and accused of things not in her jurisdiction. The masculine pushed her too far; her energy was depleted so she knew she had to move on. The feminine knew she was ready to take whatever steps were necessary to find the freedom she so dearly craved. She began to spend more time in nature with a much greater awareness of herself and her surroundings than previously.

EVERY CLOUD HAS A SILVER LINING!

She began to notice things were not as drab as she first thought. Did it really matter whether the sun was shining or the sky was blue every day? She went on to learn if she was content within herself she'd find contentment outside and this would enable her to view the world from an entirely different perspective. She began to acknowledge herself as part of a bigger reality than the one she had created. She was beginning to have a greater understanding of love, wisdom, nurturing, and justice and not just for others but herself as well.

It was then time for the masculine to let go of his tired old ways and embrace his feminine counterpart. Through this he would be able to stand on his own and walk tall. He knew the feminine would not bow to his superficial sense of superiority and cover for his inadequacies any longer. Ultimately this was all he ever really wanted but his fear of the outcome was greater than the steps he had been willing to take to arrive there.

COUNTERBALANCE

It took much soul searching for my masculine to face himself with truth and honesty to have an understanding of what it is to live in peace and harmony. His greatest decision was *how much of himself is he prepared to change to achieve this?* Nothing ventured nothing gained, so he decided to dip his toe in the water and take the steps needed to change. He was aware his old ways were not working anymore and when he was honest with himself he admitted they never had worked.

IS THIS THE LIGHT AT THE END OF THE TUNNEL?

I know I have been morally and physically corrupt in embracing the truth of myself. This is my now understanding after having to kick many goals for me to be where I am today. I have worked with universal truth to know the essence of Unconditional Love, honesty and integrity to deal with my fears and walk forward with a lighter load. It is easy for our load to get progressively heavier without our awareness. It is also incumbent on us to stop and do a stock take to know exactly where we are and what is ours to deal with. You are responsible for you as I am for me so we cannot expect another person to do for us what we are capable of doing for ourselves.

I find it's empowering to put this story on paper because now I have a deeper realisation and understanding of who I am and the journey I have taken to get myself to where I am now. I know there are still many steps to be taken and I do not fear what is around any corner. My most precious gifts have come from facing and not hiding. I am now prepared to go out there and share my little world with other people's little world's to help create a bigger and better world for us all.

I know I am not separate from anyone or anything; we are all in this together and have much to learn from then share with each other.

BE LIKE A TURTLE SLOW BUT SURE
AND LEAVE NO STONE UNTURNED
ONLY THEN CAN YOU SAY
I KNOW ME!

AFFIRMATION

I AM RESPONSIBLE FOR MY FREEDOM
SO I MUST DIVEST MYSELF OF MY SHACKLES
TO KNOW THE ESSENCE OF MY FREEDOM!

ME

My life is bound by the twine of other people's ideals and strategies
I have lived my life within the confines of these ideals and strategies
I have no idea, I did not know these ideals and
strategies were taking me nowhere
These people are invisible as is the invisible twine holding me captive
I have no idea; I did not know there is a me within the confines of nothing
Somewhere within I began to ask questions then demand answers of the invisible
Slowly, ever so slowly the twine begins to unravel
I have no idea; I do not know this person I am beginning to expose
What is left standing?
An invisible nothing, I mean nothing showing me as me
Even the invisible threads holding me captive have disappeared
I am naked, exposed as a new born
In my reality I am a newly born something
But I am lost and confused in the wilderness of nothing
Where to now?
I begin to observe what is around me
I begin to grab at fragments of anything in the hope of creating something
I open books and read words in the hope something will resonate within me
I find myself confused and floundering while trying
to grab at the light at the end of my tunnel
I begin to take pieces of everything and anything to create me
There are times I look into the mirror of my life to
find my head is everywhere and anywhere
I am like a piece of patchwork with one color here, a few poker
dots there, naughts and crosses somewhere, then triangles
and squares are maneuvering and vying for attention.
What is this rabble colluding and jumping from one extreme to another?
Who is this?
It is me!
It is the ever evolving me where nothing is permanent in a rotating universe
Subsequently I can be stripped of anything at any time until I know
When this is my only knowing I will be standing
naked with everything I will ever need!

THE PRECIPICE

The ever present precipice is trying to control my life
Fear of toppling over keeps me out of strife
Have I pushed my limits by standing on one leg?
I am robust so I will hold my ground and not beg
It's time to initiate then stay within my boundaries,
How else will I experience the wonder of my heart's desires?
I have to know the precipice is only a guide
So it is imperative for me to acknowledge then abide
Because the precipice is a reminder of my yesterdays
The distance of today's fall will be enveloped in tomorrow's haze
Tomorrow is naught but a blip on an obscure screen
Never to be fraught by my fears because they have no mean
I grapple and flounder in the dark
Only to see my light has begun to spark
Doom and gloom has now found its place
Light and love is filling this unquenched space
The precipice shows my life on the edge
For love and truth I will not hedge
I may from time to time fumble and stumble
But now I know I will not crumble
I can now acknowledge the precipice holds no fear
So it's time to shed that illusive tear!

REJECTION

REJECTION reverberates to the very core of our being. On one side of the coin is UNCONDITIONAL LOVE and on the other is REJECTION.

Our feelings of insecurity and vulnerability can be filed under the heading of *rejection*. There are also sub-headings that can fool us into playing dangerous games by delving into and using our tools of negativity. These tools can be singular or a combination of our negatives consisting of: *anger jealousy envy bitterness hate* and many more.

TOOLS OF NEGATIVITY?

These tools of negativity will manifest into negative behavioural patterns in the pretext of covering our hurt. Do we then become a human fortress and surround ourselves with a moat accessible by a hidden drawbridge? This drawbridge can be perceived as our protection from further *rejection* but for how long?

DEAL WITH ANY ISSUES YOU HAVE
RELATING TO REJECTION!

Do we set ourselves a task of self-protection by lashing out at others in whatever way we see fit? Do we allow these behavioural patterns to dictate to us the person we want the world to see? As the sharpness of our initial pain recedes do we slowly let the drawbridge down? Do we allow people to get close to us because the pain of *rejection* is receding? Will *rejection* strike when we allow ourselves to flow in the river of fun and laughter?

Rejection is personal so why do we allow other peoples *rejection* issues become a guideline for overcoming or obliterating our own? Are we prepared to give our power to anyone who we deem to have no issues of *rejection?* You have to get real and know there is no magic wand to change anything innate within you. You have to look everything in the face and know what is yours to deal with, because nobody, but nobody can change or deal with what is yours.

WHAT IS YOUR FIRST MEMORY OF REJECTION?

I believe as babies we first experience *rejection*. The feeling, the innate knowing of pain connected to *rejection* is surely ingrained in our psyche at a subconscious level. I know how defensive I have been when others have seen one of the many chinks in my armour. The resulting pain reverberates through to the very core my being to penetrate every facet of myself. *Rejection* can certainly shatter the ego because ego is based on a false sense of what it wants to believe.

We can find it difficult to acknowledge then deal with *rejection* because it goes to the essence of who we are. It's important for us to go deep within to deal with our issues because that's where they hang out. They are not interested in letting go because it means there will be a hole that needs filling. Then the dilemma is what do I fill this hole with? Try *Unconditional Love* because we know it works!

A FACADE OF ILLUSION?

Surely if we can create a façade of illusion we can open up to the reality of who the real and genuine me is. It is too easy for us to deny the essence of who we are when we are in denial. When we cannot accept our true self then live our life to its full potential we relegate ourselves to a place of emptiness. Illusion is only a facade that creates more of the same.

THE FALLOUT FROM REJECTION

Rejection presents itself to each and every one of us in a way our individual self can acknowledge and accept it. As individuals we are responsible to deal with the cause and effect *rejection* has on us if not the outcome can be catastrophic for ourself and others. We have to ask ourselves these questions because our issues of *rejection* spread far and wide.

Where does compulsive behaviour stem from?

Where do phobias stem from?

Where do addictions stem from?

Where does illness stem from?

Where does abuse stem from?

Where does cruelty stem from?

FOCUS AND HEAL!

Our focus must go right to our core to heal any wounded feelings debilitating us in our quest to be a loving caring and sharing person. We have to centre ourselves around *Unconditional Love* because nothing else will work. When we do this we bring other pieces of our jigsaw together to have some understanding of our reason for being on earth at this particular time. We have to know we have a purpose for being here. If not we will be existing and taking up space, rather than living and creating a better world for ourselves and all who follow.

RETRIBUTION AND REJECTION

With *rejection* comes retribution because no one is going to get away with *rejecting* me. Who do we then turn our retribution onto? Is it to the perpetrator or is it the self or is it someone who loves us, or is it someone unknown to us? With retribution comes bitterness and as the old saying goes – *when we throw a pebble in a lake the ripples go on and on.* So when is it time to let go of your rejection issues?

TO GROW WE MUST KEEP LEARNING!

There is no way we can justify poor behaviour when we are all here to learn and grow. We are here to heal our core issues not fling them around willy-nilly. Ultimately we are responsible for all our thoughts words and actions. How can anyone possibly know the reality of *Unconditional Love* when they are busy role playing and creating havoc in their own life as well as others? Grow up and be responsible for your own learning and do not endeavour to cover your holes with masking tape. Go within to find what you perceive is missing and fill yourself with *Unconditional Love.*

Once again I am listening to the radio as I am writing this story and the song NOBODY'S CHILD by Karen Young is being played. How appropriate this song is to this particular subject. *Nobody loves me, no mother's kisses, no father's smile; nobody loves me I'm nobody's child.* How many people would relate to these words? How many people create their world from this belief? How many people choose to live life as a product of perceived *rejection*? How many people choose to walk away from *rejection* to create a meaningful and fulfilling life?

23

There are no hard and fast rules as you have free will so *you and only you can choose to live the life you want to live.*

CHANGE THE NEGATIVITY OF REJECTION INTO A POSITIVE!

Rejection is only what we allow it to be. We can breathe life into *rejection* to create a positive reality or we can lose ourselves in the quagmire of a perceived reality.

I REITERATE THE FACT THAT *"YOU MAKE DECISIONS FOR YOU BECAUSE NO ONE ELSE CAN!"*

INTERJECTION

DEFLECT REJECTION
INJECT LOVE
CARRY YOUR BANNER INFUSED WITH
YOUR LIGHT AND LOVE
BREAK THE CHAINS OF NEGATIVITY
TO CREATE PEACE ON EARTH
FOR ALL HUMANITY

FROM FEARS TO ETERNITY

I am frozen by my fears
So why am I beholden to these fears?
What is caressing my throat?
Is it a caress or a threat?
I feel it slithering downwards
No, no not my heart I cry
I feel its grip
It's probing then pulling and pushing
Its tentacles are surrounding and squeezing
I am now drowning in my own blood
My ears are pounding
My eyes are congealed
Slowly my body is awash with nothingness
Anguish is threatening to be my master
I know I am responsible *but*?
I am holding onto my fears as if my life depends on them
I had to blame you then you as my courage was hiding under my fears
How much more pain do I need to endure?
I can now feel my fears rise and separate
Shards of these fears are now screaming for release
Yes please detach from my being
Yes I say I embrace you all because now it is my time
Time to love and nurture me
I am now shedding my suit of destitution
To walk into the arms of Unconditional Love
With my fears melting like snow under the hot sun
I can now walk into my life and take it by the hand
With the knowing of whoever I was, I am not!
For I am now creating me moment by precious moment.

WHY BLAME SOCIETY?

WHO IS TO BLAME?

I was having a conversation with a young man who is well on the way to completing a university degree in psychiatry. This young man blames society for all his foibles and in doing so believes this entitles him to take no responsibility for his actions. From his perspective he is a product of other generation's creations. He blames society for his attitude to life and behaviour by believing society is responsible for his partying and irresponsible ways. I asked where responsibility for himself began and society's ended? He was not going to be budged from his mind set as somewhere along his life's journey he took on this belief to suit his purpose as was indicated by his attitude.

CYNICISM UNDERMINES WHAT?

I responded to this in my usual manner. I went home and pondered on all he had said. This young man worked part time to finance his living expenses. Over a number of months I had a number of conversations with him. He has a friendly and laid back manner but I began to see a cynicism in him belying his years. I enjoyed standing back and observing his banter with people and it seemed the more familiar he became to me the more cynical I perceived him to be.

When he asked people his famous question *"what sort of a day have you had"* he received many and varied answers and reactions. Some people ignored the question while others were waiting to be asked so they could burden someone else with their lot in life. I'm sure this all helped him in his chosen career.

LOVELY DAY LADY

I attracted his attention because I would always say I had a wonderful day and life was great. He would question me on my motives because from his perspective life was not always wonderful. Everyone has their ups and downs so why was I always happy. I would say *"I am happy because I have the choice of being happy or not. It just happens I choose to be happy no matter what is going on in my life as only I am responsible for me and my attitude to my life"*.

LEARNING IS INFINITE!

Whenever I would see him he had a smile touched with cynicism planted on his face. I enjoyed our banter because he was teaching me as much about myself as I was learning about him. He is representative of many younger people who blame the previous generations for their lot in life. They then live their lives according to the belief of *do what you want when you want and blow the consequences.* Self justification for anything is only a perspective created from an illusion that's trying to delude us from our truth.

WHO'S PASSING THE BUCK?

This line of thinking must take a huge weight off anyone's laden shoulders because blaming previous generations gives them permission to live their life as they please. Who does have to take responsibility for the actions of people who are in denial? Who has told these people they are not responsible for themselves? This is such a cop out of self responsibility. It's not okay to blame previous generations? If this was our reality we would all be imbeciles who sell their free will to justify irresponsibility.

RULES SHOULD GUIDE, NOT DICTATE!

I could not agree with the attitude he directed at society. In society there are rules and guidelines but it's up to the individual as to how we regulate our lives then conform to our own rules.

Humans are very selective in how they see life so have a tendency to break rules. Some people seem to get a sense of achievement and freedom when going against society. How many people believe rules are meant to be broken?

BE RESPONSIBLE!

If you asked these people, *"what is it you want, what part of your life do you assume is being neglected by other people?"* They will most likely stammer and stumble because people usually say these things for a reaction but when you confront them they don't know how to answer. These people can get caught up in the drama of gaining attention so would prefer you leave them alone.

We sell ourselves short whenever we put what's ours out to other people because *as the law of attractions says, it will find its way back to you!*

WHERE IS TRUTH?

There are many representatives of society who come together with their own agendas. They do so without respecting individuals then create rules and regulations for control. They say *this is how it is, this is what you must do, this is how you should think, you must follow what we say and if we are wrong too bad.* Somehow somewhere truth gets buried outside of ourselves because our inner knows.

WHO RULES WHO?

Who are the conglomerate of individuals who set rules and regulations for us to adhere to? Who are these people who steal our power then tell us what we should know. I don't know about you but I have very little understanding of what our politicians are trying to say to us. I know there are some wonderful people in positions of power who really care and work for the people. On the other hand there are many who get caught up in their own ego and use their self power for control.

WHERE DOES EGO FIT IN?

Why would one person want to control another? It can only be in their best interest because it surely isn't in mine. When rules are created by people to be followed by other people there will be an attachment of ego. Ego is not natural it is learned.

FEAR OF RULES

Many rules are set to protect us from ourselves or so we are told. Fear lays waiting deep within like a coiled snake readying itself to attack. Fear masquerades as any number of negatives while promising to deliver a more rewarding life. When we are not in touch with the realness of ourselves we grab at everything fear has to offer in the belief we are in charge of our lives. *I am in charge of my own life and no one can tell me what I can or cannot do.*

When rules are created our fear factor is alerted as there will be consequences if we do not abide. When we set our own rules out of respect for ourselves and other people there will be no need to follow any other than our own.

HONESTY SHOULD BE OUR ONLY POLICY

How much courage does it take for me to be true to myself? How much courage does it take for me not to emulate my peers? Only I the individual can answer this because it goes to the core of who and what I am. Unless I come from my place of honesty truth and integrity I will never treat you with the same.

We all have the wherewithal to make positive decisions to create a difference in our own world. It is not up to us to blame society for anything because society is made up of individuals who all have the gift of free will.

AM I RESPONSIBLE FOR MY THOUGHTS?

You are not responsible for your thoughts but you are responsible what you do with them. Thoughts come and go like people through a revolving door. No one takes any notice until movement is halted then people are stuck with nowhere to go. When our thoughts get stuck they begin to take form to create a life of their own. This can be powerful when we believe everything this thought is telling us.

This thought can be telling me so, and so does not like me and has been spreading rumours around about me. Then I can ring a mutual friend and ask her has she heard any rumours relating to me. When she says no, do I believe her? You can see where this is going. When you do not know yourself you are insecure so will believe everything your thoughts want to tell you. No matter what you may think you are totally responsible for the way you behave from a thought.

PURE THOUGHTS CREATE HARMONY!

Harmony does create pure and positive thoughts. Negative thoughts can feed *anger vindictiveness bitterness* and every other negative feeling. Positive thoughts are uplifting.

Oh isn't it a great day life's fantastic I'm on top of the world. Then a negative thought presents itself to you and everything changes. Why has this happened to me, I am so unlucky. As soon as I begin to feel happy something always happens to make me grumpy. Remember you are the only one who can put your thoughts into perspective so take charge of your life to create harmony for yourself.

AN ILL WIND DOES BLOW!

Ill thoughts manifest illness within the body. If you don't deal with something or someone who causes you grief it stays in your body until you do. Then more thoughts keep adding to the pile you have not as yet dealt with. Eventually your body gets tired of holding everything in so will become heavy from carrying around the extra weight. Then due to your body not being able to release your issues it begins to break down to cause you pain. Your body is telling you to wake up and release what is not working for you, if not you will have a lot more on your plate to deal with.

WHAT IS LACKING IN YOUR LIFE?

Do not put out to others what you do not want in your own life. If you believe something is lacking in your life take responsibility and change your thinking. You are your own creation so if you are not happy change. Take responsibility for any illness you have within because you are a powerful being who creates you through your thoughts.

When you live your truth you detach yourself from others and their dramas. You do not need to attach yourself to other people's roller coaster rides as it's enough being on your own. The bottom line is that you are on your own so create the life you want. Change whatever needs changing for you to live your truth with integrity. Your personal choice is for you to make and not society.

ORACLE

I Create my own Rules because I want Me to Live My Life
with Unconditional Love Light Truth and Honesty.
I Affirm I will join my Truth with your Truth for a One Consciousness of Truth.
There are no Rules or Regulations Greater than the ones I
have Created to help Build a Better World for us All!
We are all in this together, Individuals Swimming
our way through the Sea of Life.

WHAT IS NORMAL?

I am confused as to what is *normal*?
I have been told on more than one occasion that
it is prudent to be seen as *normal*!
I have a lovely psychologist who tells me she loves colors but every
session I have had with her she has worn predominantly *black*.
Does a person who is need of a psychologist want to be
confronted by *black* or the *vibrancy of colors*?
Does my individuality compete with what is decreed to be *normal*?
Where has this word *normal* come from?
Has *normal* been birthed from a fear of being out of step with the masses?
Must we think, eulogise, criticise, evaluate then walk
in each other's footsteps to be *normal*.
My house is different to your house so whose house is *normal*?
How many children do I need to have to be considered as *normal*?
There are many people throughout history who have given a great deal
of themselves unconditionally and are celebrated for their wonderful
achievements, but society still relates to them as being *normal* why?
Do I feel secure in the land of the *normal*?
Where do we retreat to when I don't want to be seen as *normal*?
Should *normal* only relate to a setting on a washing machine?
I must admit I have never met anyone who is *normal*
because individuals have individual characteristics.
In my finite wisdom I believe there is no person
who should ever be labeled *normal*.
If you know differently please enlighten me!
Some characteristics of ours can be similar but
this doesn't mean they are *normal*.
I do not use the word *normal* relating to people because
I believe they deserve respect and *normal* tells me
nothing about the uniqueness of an individual.

NORMAL IS ONLY AS NORMAL IS!

COURAGE TO CHANGE

How many people say they want to change?
How many people only want to change aspects of themselves?
What does change mean for me an individual?
How deep within the self are we prepared go to instigate change?

CHANGE

I can say I want to change for as long as it takes for the cows to come home but unless I am prepared to act on my words *nothing* will change. When I say *I want to change because nothing I seem to do works for me anymore. I* need to have a picture in my mind of what I want my life to look like. It's no use saying I want to change then do nothing to bring it about.

Many people are trapped in a life they believe is not of their own making. They can then say "I want to change because *I do not want to continue walking this path as everything is too hard". Surely I deserve better than what I am experiencing.* We cannot change unless we have the intention to create a better life for ourselves. Do we instigate change when we come to the point of saying, enough is enough?

ACCESS YOUR COURAGE BECAUSE IT MAY BE IN HIDING

Am I foolish enough to believe by saying abracadabra everything will change? Am I foolish enough to believe these words will bring in the new when I have not had the courage to leave the old behind? Change has more connotations attached to it than any other word in the dictionary. It means I have to throw out all my old thoughts, words, actions and habits to allow in the new.

It takes tremendous courage and effort for me to change because I have to face myself to bring about any changes I require for my life. I have to change my thinking conditioning from birth programming from *religions teachers parents families communities cultures and society* in general. There are *no short cuts* or *back doors* when we truly want to change. I have to look every aspect of myself in the eye then acknowledge it is a part of me. I have to look in the mirror and know the person looking back at me is me and change can only come through me. I have to know I am the most important person in my life.

I must ask myself, *"what benefits will I get when I change me?"*
I am the only person who can answer this question because it's only about me and how I want to live my life!

Living my life for other people is self-serving especially when I have no real idea of who they are. When I give my attention to other people I am denying me of fulfilling my needs and wants. I can say *"I am okay, everything is great, my life is wonderful as long as long as I keep busy doing things for you."* I then need to ask myself who needs me more than I need me?

HELP YOURSELF SO YOU CAN ENJOY
THE SMORGASBOARD OF LIFE

Who does need me more than I need me? Whose needs am I really fulfilling? I may delude myself into believing I am *doing* for other people but what about taking the time to *be here* for me? We are all here together on earth for our own learning so I need to stop deluding myself I am here for anyone else. I will only ever be here for others when I know how to be here for me.

COURAGE COME OUT WHEREVER YOU ARE

Courage is an asset accessible to each and every one of us. Due to our patterning and conditioning I may have to reach deep within myself to grab hold of it to bring it into my line of vision. I will then know I have to change my life's course because whatever worked previously is surely not working now. Realistically, it never really was working but I kept telling myself the same old story hoping for a new ending.

People do not want to change when they fear *rocking the boat* then having to face the consequences. What we neglect to see is we all have free will so we control the rudder steering our boat.

I have to choose how far and in what direction I will take. I have to know when I make the decision to change I will be taken out of my comfort zone.

How many people are prepared to leave their comfort zone to pack their bags then rough it?

Do you see yourself as placid? If so is this because you will not make a decision then find yourself giving your opinion through fear of being ridiculed? When asked for your opinion do you feel equipped to give the answer you believe is expected of you? Do you feel vulnerable and insecure when you have to voice your opinion?

BULLY OR VICTIM?

How and when would a bully find the courage to change?

How and when would a victim find the courage to change?

When I was being bullied at school and then at work I never contemplated change because I believed I was getting what I deserved. I could not see beyond my pain to even begin to change. *I was worthless I was insipid I was fat I did not have an engaging personality I had pimples I was not smart* and so I was getting what I deserved.

Is bullying becoming more prevalent or is it more in our face now? Are people talking about it more? Has it shifted from the home into school yards, streets and any other places people congregate? Is it due to mobile phones or the internet? How many people are bullied in the work place from colleagues or bosses then keep it to themselves because they are too embarrassed or afraid of losing their job to report it?

I knew a man who worked for the same company as me who was a bully. He was in charge of some of the apprentices and was well known for his bullying tactics. Eventually the reason for his bullying came out. He was a short man who had a wife who was bigger than him and apparently she would bully him. Instead of dealing with it he brought it to work and took it out on the men who worked under him.

A victim has learned to be a victim for many and varied reasons. A victim must realise the door of positivity is closed when the door of negativity is open. You may hide but the time will come when you need to stand up for yourself. I know it's difficult but somewhere within you have to find then listen to the voice of positivity. This will tell you just how *strong intelligent diverse caring*

35

giving and loveable you are. The more you listen to this inner voice the greater your courage will be to bring about change in your life.

Whether you are a bully or a victim you can change. The only thing stopping you is your fear of yourself. *Fear of change, fear of confronting you, fear of living, fear upon fear upon fear* holding your life to ransom. Your fear is dictating to you as to how you live your life, who to listen to and who to believe. Whether you acknowledge it or not your fears are locked within you. Release your fears and set them free so you will know the real meaning of freedom.

WHERE DO I FIT IN?

There are many dramas played out in families, society and life in general. We have to be courageous to look at and deal with the many aspects of ourselves. We cannot look to others for our answers as they are too busy looking for their own. People may relay messages to you about you but it comes from their knowing and not yours.

How do you feel or react when you hear negatives relating to yourself? If you are angry you have to ask yourself then answer honestly as to *why am I angry*? Anger can be a natural response when trying to hide the parts of yourself not fitting someone else's criteria. Anger sets off your defence mechanisms so you allow your controlled senses to overtake common sense. How long do you allow your anger to control you before you find the courage to deal with it and change? *ANGER = WEAKNESS, COURAGE = STRENGTH!*

MY BATTLE WITH CHANGE

I kept walking the same path even though I was faced with the same old hazards. Why did I do this? What was it going to take for me to change course? I tried to conquer every aspect of my life but I seemed to create another barrier for myself. Do I walk over every person who has ever walked over and trampled me into the ground to appease my need for revenge? Am I here to avenge the deeds of all who have walked this path before me? It's time to wake up look and listen and give your path a wide berth so I can walk my path.

Last week Howard accused me of sabotaging my happiness. I was affronted because I didn't know how to deal with this accusation. I realised he was showing me exactly what I needed rather than what I wanted to see. I allowed my pride to raise its ugly head in attempting to convince me otherwise. Deep within I knew he was right but my indignant self was not ready acquiesce. He clearly articulated his reasoning but I was still in the house of denial.

GOOD TEACHER, POOR STUDENT

I was presented with a teacher who taught me many things about myself and life. She had the ability to reach inside of me and pull out my dramas for everyone to see. I felt totally exposed by her methods on many occasions. I felt raw and vulnerable and my fear of someone seeing the *real me* was confronting. I spent years trying to work through *my stuff* and it was not easy when things I saw in other people were actually my own. I had to own and deal with every part of myself if not I would still be back there beating out the some old tune.

MY FIGHT TO CHANGE

I was stuck in my self made swamp. I needed to access the courage to pull myself out, clean myself off and walk forward with strong confident steps. I was always looking for someone to rescue me rather than me rescuing me. The time came when I had to fight for me to change me because no one could do for me what I wasn't prepared to do for myself.

The way in which I dealt with change in myself is through the understanding and belief that I am a part of all there is. I had to go deep within to help guide me in whatever way I needed to bring about change in my life. Many times I asked for a sign to affirm me I was on the right track. My confirmation was in my now awareness to know what I was looking for, then to see it.

Doors began to open and every change I made brought with it more freedom until I finally became my friend. The people closest to me had seen glimpses of the beautiful me so they knew how much work I had to do to pull every part together for me to be whole. When one person decides to change, then implements the changes needed, there can be a domino effect on other family members.

I have changed and no doubt continue changing and evolving while residing on earth. I used to think I knew what love meant but I now realise I knew the word but not the feeling. I was oblivious to real and not perceived knowing of beauty. I was surrounded by it but I never saw. Once the flame of love ignited inside me I knew I never wanted it to be extinguished.

FEAR OF CHANGE

Why do we fear change? Is it because we like the old that's not working for us now? Is it because we have learned to accept mediocrity? Is it because our *friends* may not accept us anymore? Is it because we love the person who is reflected back to us when we look in a mirror? Is it because it's just too difficult? Is it because you believe your life is working for you when in actual fact it's not? Is it because you like the familiar nothing? You have to know what is for you as I have had know what is for me.

POSITIVES OF CHANGE

Change brings new people into your life. You will find a helping hand, a kind word or a piece of a puzzle falls into place when you need it. You have to know things are exactly as they are meant to be for your learning and growth so everything is on track. You have to trust that it's all in your own.............
DIVINE TIMING.

Do not ever let anything or anyone hold you back because you are playing for the highest stakes of all. You are playing for you and only you can create your life for you. If you stumble it's okay as long as you keep walking forward. If you fall it's also okay as long as you pick yourself up and keep walking.

Change can only enhance your life when coming from the intention of integrity. You can do no wrong when every step you take is leading you to you!

ANECDOTE

CHANGE COMES FROM WITHIN
SO LIVE YOUR LIFE AS ONLY YOU CAN
CHANGE OPENS UP A FOUNTAIN OF LOVE
SO ALLOW YOUR LOVE TO OVERFLOW
AND TOUCH EVERY PERSON IN YOUR LIFE
UNLEASH YOUR COURAGE TO CHANGE
THEN YOU WILL KNOW!

CHANGE

Change for change sake, is no change
Change to give your life meaning, is change
Change taking you to your higher purpose, is change
Change aligning body, mind and spirit, is change
Change to create a life with purpose, is change
Change to know and live *unconditional love,* is change
Change to embrace the people in your life, is change
Change to communicate your truth, is change
Change comes in many and various forms!
Change is mandatory for us to live a life filled with joy and harmony
So why is change so difficult?
Is it because the word change without action has no meaning?
Activating change begins with intention!
Change can be fraught with fears
But without change fears win
Change is not giving our thoughts substance
So what's left when substance is removed from a thought?
There is nothing!
Only when we acknowledge this there will be no need to change
Because we will have implemented our changes!

BOUNDARIES

ARE HUMANS PROGRAMMED TO SET BOUNDARIES?

Due to our programming we learn the basics for our survival are through control resulting in either positive or negative behaviour. Boundaries can be set through *fear, selfishness, insecurity, illusion, love, happiness* or anything the self can find to build its foundation on.

We create boundaries for ourselves then create another set of boundaries for other people. Nonetheless, whether the act is a conscious or subconscious one the outcome can still be the same. Boundaries are created to hold our guard in place then can translate into protection from any ill wind that blows our way.

HOW IMPORTANT IS OUR PERSONAL SPACE?

We learn from an early age what is mine, what belongs to me. We then create boundaries around what we believe belongs to us so others will not intrude on our personal space. I learnt, to my detriment from a very early age a strategy I put in place backfired and left me in tears with a lesson I thought at the time would destroy me.

DID THE DEVAS AND FAIRIES HAVE A FEAST AT MY EXPENSE?

When I was very young I received some lollies for my birthday and I didn't want to share them with my siblings. I carefully put them under the cabbages dad was growing in our abundant vegetable garden.

The next day all hell broke loose because when I went to retrieve my lollies I couldn't find them. I was distraught and blamed all and sundry until I came to grips with the reality of having put them in an unfortunate place for me, but not for the night creatures who resided in our garden. I certainly learned my lesson because I never put any chocolates or lollies outside again.

BOUNDARIES WITHIN BOUNDARIES

Boundaries were set by the people who founded our country to distinguish what belonged to who. In doing so the country was then divided into states then more boundaries were created when the states were divided into cities, towns and municipalities. Then these were further divided into farms, house blocks and so on. There are boundaries created within boundaries and then more are created to fulfil our need for privacy.

WHY DO WE NEED TO BE CONTROLLED?

We see signs erected telling us *Private Property Keep Out, Do Not Enter, No Parking* and the list is growing every day.

What do people do when pushed into a corner by rules and signs telling us what we can and cannot do? Many people rebel, and then find themselves regulated by more rules, signs and inevitably more boundaries. The more boundaries created means that more boundaries are needed to keep us either in or out.

The people who believe they have power over the majority will do whatever they can with whatever means they can to control. These people are there to work for and with us but they don't. Some certainly do but most don't. Somehow a position of power seems to give a person reason to lie and distort the truth to suit themselves. A once engaging person will go to any lengths to be unaccountable. It's not my fault, it is out of my hands, no comment and so it goes.

We are constantly faced with boundaries when driving a vehicle due to ever changing speed limits and signs for this, that and the other. We know the consequences of not adhering to them so the choice as always is ours to make. Our awareness and patience gets tested when we know there are cameras waiting to photograph us doing the *wrong thing*. We know we cannot beat a system where rules have been set to protect us from ourselves.

ARE YOU ACCOUNTABLE?

We are all accountable because we acquiesced to allow boundaries to be set when we could not dignify ourselves by setting inner boundaries. The big picture shows we are all bound together when living on earth. We are not separate as every one of our actions has a reaction.

WHAT DOES OWNERSHIP MEAN FOR YOU?

Greed seems to have taken over from caring and sharing. It's now imperative for me the individual to declare what belongs to me then erect signs decreeing the same. More and more I hear of what is hers, his, yours and mine and gone is the acknowledgment of what is ours. In reality we ultimately only own ourselves so this is where our responsibility begins and ends. When we learn to be true to ourselves we will be true to other people and signs will not be necessary.

Society only reflects the inconsistencies of boundaries we create within then outside of ourselves. When our boundaries are based on the pure emotions of *Unconditional Love truth respect honour justice caring sharing and trust* we will know we have created a place within that serves us well. Then I will have no need for boundaries.

HOW PRECIOUS IS YOUR FREE WILL?

The world spirit will never discriminate between any individual because it knows we are not separate. No one is more or less loved than any other whether it be human animal plant insect and ultimately the whole of Mother Earth. Humans have put themselves above all else because we think we can due to us having the gift of free will.

There will always be some fallout from every decision we make. We have the ability to take ourselves to the highest of highs conversely we can allow ourselves to be sucked into the very depth of our being. We are driving our own life so we can choose to acknowledge and take responsibility for our uniqueness or not.

Only by giving and sharing our love with others will we know how to receive and accept love without any conditions attached. Love is pure so why would anyone want to put boundaries or conditions around it. In our uniqueness we are all vessels of love so when we create boundaries we have to know and understand these boundaries are in reality an illusion.

WE ARE IT ALL, WE JUST NEED REMINDING!

Do we fear our capacity to love believe and trust because we deem ourselves vulnerable and not in control of our life? Do we then find ourselves putting our expectations on other people to fill a void we have created? When we believe in ourselves and our capacity to be everything, expectation will be nonexistent.

We have to know every boundary we negotiate is a part of ourselves because if it was not we would not see it. We have to understand the power we have and the responsibility that goes with it. When our outer marries up with our inner self there will be no need of boundaries against anyone or anything.

When our true self emerges we will be consummate in Unconditional Love Light and Truth because there will be no boundaries.

SUMMARY

WHEN WE ARE MASTERS OF OURSELVES
WE WILL BE VESSELS OF TRUTH AND LOVE
BOUNDARIES WILL NEVER BE REQUIRED
SO ANY QUESTION RELATING TO WHO I AM
WILL BE ANSWERED WITH
I AM EVERYWHERE
I AM IT ALL
I AM!

AM I DREAMING?

Am I dreaming?
If not, where am I?
I am surrounded by beauty
I know beauty is in the eye of the beholder
BUT, this is beautiful
Surely it cannot be a dream
Trees and plants are whispering their secrets from long ago
There standing before me in its magnificence is an albino magpie
This magpie unreservedly acknowledges its beauty
So why can't I?
The breeze caresses my hair with love and respect
The bird song breaks through the stillness of the moment
Am I dreaming?
If not, where am I?
I feel rested and rosy as I wipe remnants of sleep from my eyes
I am fully awake and not dreaming
I now know,
My beauty is not in the eye of any beholder
My beauty is in me!

OSCAR AND FREEDOM

OSCAR'S STORY

Oscar's story began June 2, 2004. My daughter and I had lunch together and due to her having a dinner engagement that night I dropped her off at Howard's business which is a specialised brake and clutch workshop. As Howard's workshop was in the vicinity of Melbourne's CBD it was convenient for her to travel to the venue from there.

FREEDOM IN A BOX?

When we arrived at the workshop there was a slight commotion as we were to learn a budgerigar had flown into the premises and landed in a cardboard box. The workers were quite perplexed because they did not know what to do. One worker already had a bird, a number of dogs and lived approximately two hour's drive from the work place so did not want to subject the bird to the long drive home.

I was asked whether it was possible for me to take the bird home so I agreed this would be a good idea. There were no houses in the immediate vicinity of the business so it would have been futile to try to find out where it came from. By this time the bird had entrenched himself in what was then was its new home and it certainly was in no hurry to move. My only concern about taking it home was the fact I have a cat who is totally mesmerised by birds.

WHAT CAN $100 BUY?

Astral the cat may be mesmerised by birds but that's as far as it goes because he is handicapped in his ability to catch any birds due to having only three legs (this is another story). Howard gave me $100 to buy the necessities for our new family member. I found a pet shop and went in it to find myself confronted by many and varied bird trappings.

When I was younger my family had birds at various times. In those days almost everybody had a birdcage of sorts in their backyard, but not so these days. I was confronted with an abundance of cages. There were large cages as well as a variety of medium and small ones. Some were bright and colorful others black and white. In my dilemma I chose a lovely big green cage as the bird was predominantly green, so I believed I was in the ball park of bird fashion.

WAS GREEN THE COLOUR OF THE DAY?

An assistant spotted me and rubbed her hands together because I had that green and gullible look. When I told the saleswoman my plight she began to run here and there picking bits and pieces of every necessity required for the comfort of this little bird.

My head was spinning as the counter began to fill with the essentials this bird obviously needed. I was beginning to realise this bird knew exactly what it was doing when it flew into the workshop. I was beginning to see a bigger picture where nothing was in my hands. I had no control of any outcome (but realistically I did because this bird would now rely on me protecting him and fulfilling his basic needs).

FRILLS, SPILLS AND CHILLS!

The assistant gave me instructions on every essential contraption sitting on the counter. There were sprays and drops, a swing a trapeze artist from a circus would be proud of. Then there was the mirror that had everything a small green bird could ever want attached to it. Following were the toys it would need so it wouldn't get bored, and then on top of it all was the food. I remembered previously there was only one brand of birdseed but I was soon to realise those days were well and truly gone. There was food to beef it up and keep it healthy and happy as well as the everyday budgie seed. We used to put sand at the bottom of a bird cage but not so in these days of enlightenment. Now we need a special grit that I am sure works far better than the sand and dirt ever did.

ANOTHER $75 LATER!

I was soon to realise the $100 Howard gave me clearly would not cover the pile sitting on the counter. Fortunately I had my friend the credit card handy so another $75 later I walked with my purchases out of the pet shop. When I arrived home the juggling act began. Somehow I had to get the bird into his new home with all his bits and pieces in place and at the same time appease my cat and dog.

CONTROLLING BEDLAM

The cat (Astral) and dog (Jasper) were not as accommodating or willing to share in my patience. I found myself walking a fine line but the outcome was worthwhile. The cat was crying then the dog alternated between crying and barking so I knew it was imperative for me to keep my cool and carry out my task with as little fuss as possible.

Eventually the bird was set up in his new home and to my chagrin he did not care for all the accessories he was supposed to need. He was on a cabinet well out of reach of our cat but this is did not deter him. He used every strategy he possibly could to get to his nemesis the bird. The dog tried in vain to help the cat as love and caring for each other (this beautiful and moving relationship is a separate story that I have included in this book so I will not elaborate on it in now) is second to none.

OSCAR THE COMMUNICATOR

The bird's cage was close to my computer so we often communicated when I was writing. The first night we had it I asked it to tell me his name then Oscar came to me very strongly. This was quite amusing for me because somewhere along the line I have a quirky relationship with Oscar Wilde. I cannot claim to have studied or to have read many of his works but I feel I have a connection to his eccentricity.

OSCAR AND FREEDOM

Oscar was absolutely beautiful so it was a joy to have him (it must be a male if his name is Oscar) as a member of our family. He loved his life as he *sang talked chirped ate* and *slept* when it suited him.

Initially Astral would sit and watch him and cry. Then maneuver himself into a position to enable him to get to this intruder who was making his life a misery. Numerous times Astral attempted to jump up to Oscar's cage and numerous times he landed face first on the floor. This action did not deter Oscar from what he was doing so I realised he had no fear and felt totally safe.

CAGED BIRDS, I DON'T THINK SO

I have to say as I *evolved* I decided in my infinite wisdom birds should be free and not kept in a cage. Well I have fallen on my sword so many times you think I would have learned from these experiences. *But no* I do not seem to have learned very much at all. Oscar had his chance to be free (this was my interpretation of freedom) and was not interested in my idea of freedom.

I realised when Oscar flew into the box in the workshop he was free. He was fearful not free when he was flying in the open because this made him a prey to predators. There are many predators when a bird is bred specifically for the purpose of being a pet. He carried proof of this because he had slight scarring where he was pecked while he was (to my way of thinking) free.

OSCAR DANCES TO HIS OWN TUNE!

Oscar showed me every day just how free he was because he danced to his own tune. Oscar sang, chirped and danced without the need of an audience for approval or accolades. His freedom came from our love to allow him to be who he was by respecting his freedom. He had no need to leave his cage because everything he could possibly ever want was within him.

OFF THE MARK AGAIN?

I used to think to be free I had to get away and be a part of nature. I now realise there are many people who are like Oscar. They don't have the resources to go out to nature on a whim to rejuvenate themselves. He taught me we have everything we need within us and it is up to us to know and accept this reality. My idea of freedom is to sit in nature and leave my rubbish with her instead of dealing with it. Freedom is innate within each and every one of us so embrace it we must.

HOW FREE IS FREEDOM?

Until we know freedom from within we will never know the true meaning what it can be for us. Freedom comes from dealing with every one of our negative issues then healing the same. We cannot expect any other person to take our baton from us then run with it down our path. Our journey is ours so we are responsible and accountable for our own life.

We need to ask ourselves what is my idea of freedom? How will I know when I am free? Where do I need to be to be free? Do I want to experience freedom? How much am I prepared to give of and for yourself to be free? Believe me there are no excuses as we all have the tools to bring this reality into our life so *only I* can block the process.

PERFECTION OF FREEDOM!

Last Monday was a public holiday so Howard and I went to visit a very dear friend who has built a two storey house where her privacy is assured. She is high up on a mountain where we could see for miles around. This woman's closest neighbours are two eagles and many kangaroos. Her property is vast and the vegetation surrounding her is what I consider as beautifully Australian.

FREEDOM IN A STORM!

The house has not long been built and consists of many windows allowing our friend to be one with the outside world. Last week when we were there the wind was howling and the black clouds were scuttling across the sky at a ferocious pace. The rain found its way into the house through cracks not properly sealed. Nothing could detract us from the beauty and perfection of nature. It was fiercely tearing away at the house and threatening to blow it into oblivion, but we knew we were safe.

PERFECTION OF NATURE!

This was a very moving and powerful experience for us all. I then understood in those moments the true meaning of freedom. My life was in the hands of a powerful and ferocious aspect of nature and I felt safe. Nature dances and sways to her own tune as well as all of *God's* creatures. Humans keep looking for more outside rather than counting their blessings for what they already have.

WHEN ARE WE FREE?

We have everything we need at our fingertips. This does not seem to deter people from dipping their fingers into someone else's kitbag to take what they think they need. Our free will allows us to choose for ourselves. We seem to have a need to change things we perceive are not important in our lives. To change we have to look at the parts of ourselves that are not integral to us living a full and loving life.

POSITIVES AND NEGATIVES OF FREEDOM?

Yes we are free! We can hide our secrets and indiscretions behind a façade then claim innocence while perceiving it to be our truth. I am free to lie, cheat and treat people as poorly as befits what I consider to be my right. I have no boundaries so my freedom extends to wherever I choose and if it encroaches on someone else's freedom, too bad, tell someone who cares.

FREEDOM TO KILL, ABUSE AND MAIME?

How many people have this attitude? How many people know the truth of freedom? We are confronted time and again through the media of people who use their free will to take another person's freedom away from them. People are abused, killed, maimed because others believe it's their right to cause atrocities.

We hear of freedom fighters but do they have any idea of the reality of freedom. If people did understand the truth of freedom they would not be fighting for it, they would be living it. Since when have guns and freedom been relative to each other? Unless we know freedom within we will never live a life free from the underlying fear of outer freedom.

FRAGMENTED FREEDOM?

On the other hand how many people stand back while their freedom disintegrates before their very eyes. Then they expect someone else to pick up their pieces and put their life back together. We learn nothing when other people use some string and a prayer to hold our life together. Our learning is us bringing the fragments of ourselves together to be a whole person.

WE ARE MASTERS OF OUR OWN DESTINY AND WE ARE THE POWER OF OURSELVES.

FREEDOM IN THE WILDERNESS?

As I am writing this story I hear a voice calling me from the wilderness so I bring myself back into my body to try and track down the source. After a few moments I realise Howard is the source and he is still in bed enjoying a much needed sleep in. When I walked into the bedroom I find him in a very animated state. He is relating to me a vivid dream he had just woken from.

From a distance he could see children being dropped from a building four to five storey's high. They were being caught by men waiting below, and then they would be dropped even further with other men waiting to catch them. He felt it was like a fire drill but these people were doing it for fun. He felt himself move closer only to see the fear the children were experiencing and no one was saying or doing anything.

He spoke out by saying how stupid these people were for doing this to the children. Howard is not a very tall man so when he objected to their actions he was threatened by a man much bigger than he was. Then an even bigger man spoke out in Howard's defence by saying other people around were aware of it being wrong but they did not speak out.

The crowd was milling around and joined together in praising Howard and saying he was a hero. He said he was not and the real hero was the man who supported him as he was prepared to stand up and be counted when others were contented to sit on their hands. This man then realised he was more powerful than the man who threatened Howard. Howard told the milling crowd they were also more powerful the man with the threats. The dream finished with the hero shaking hands with the other man and letting him know that he was the more powerful of the two.

ABUSING FREEDOM?

I wonder what significance this is for me. I sit and ponder on the connection Howard's dream has to my story. To me his dream was predominantly about freedom and children. Their freedom had been taken away from them when the choice was made by other people to use them in the appalling way they did. These children had no control over any outcome because their safety was reliant on the ability of the men catching them.

Then there was the freedom others exercised to condemn the *so called fun* these people were having at the children's expense. One voice from the wilderness can awaken the many who are waiting for someone else to lead the way. When we sit back and wait for someone else to make the first move we are admitting we are powerless. Why are we fearful of standing up and expressing our point of view? We have to ask ourselves what is the worst thing that can happen to us when we put ourselves forward?

FREEDOM TO MOVE FORWARD

Unless we continuously move forward we will never know our personal freedom. Well it is time for us to get to know ourselves and what freedom is for me. We are not interested in other peoples ideas and views as only mine can be important for me. You may try to hide behind every barrier you come across and that's okay as long as you come out striding forward and do not look back.

The freedom of the world is the responsibility of every person on this earth at any one time. There is no room for ifs and buts or excuses. Someone or many someone's have to stand tall and shout the messages of *peace freedom love truth harmony* and *joy* to the ones who lack the foresight to do so.

There are no tomorrows, there is only *now*. *Now*, this moment we have to take charge of our own lives and our freedom because tomorrow will always be too late. Emulate Oscar if you have to and find yourself a cage (wherever that may be) then sit still and understand what freedom is for you.

It is not being caught up in the dramas of other people and trying to solve their problems, *it is about you*. It is about setting your own boundaries to allow you to have the freedom you need to inspire others to do the same. You cannot rely on another person for anything because your learning comes from relying on yourself.

Oscar lived with us for two years and taught us that outer freedom begins with inner freedom. He loved sitting outside in his cage singing his song of praise for nature. He brought an innocence and freshness into our lives for which we will be forever grateful for. He had no expectations and his every need was met. This should be a valuable lesson for us all.

I know as I am sitting here revising this story ten years on his spirit is still with us. He is free to fly with the abundance of birds who frequent our now property. He left his mark on us and I know we will meet up again one day.

OSCAR'S ODE TO FREEDOM!

I AM ON EARTH TO KNOW AND LIVE FREELY
FEEDOM IS MY RIGHT
I AM A POWERFUL PART OF NATURE
SO I MUST NEVER ENTERTAIN THE IDEA
OF ME NOT DESERVING FREEDOM
BECAUSE YOU DO
AS I DO!

KANGAROOS DANCE OF LOVE

Last Thursday morning I woke up at around 6.30am by myself as Howard stayed in Melbourne for the night. I was resting then decided to do a meditation when my nose was blocked so I reached over for my handkerchief. As I was doing this I looked out the window and witnessed a sight I was so humbled by and in awe of, unfolding before my eyes.

I will preface this by saying we have a family of kangaroos who are a part of our extended family. When Howard and I first moved to this location there was a father and mother kangaroo who had a joey in her pouch. I used telepathy to let them know we respected them and wanted them to feel free as we would never hurt them. Howard was just Howard in showing them gentleness and respect. With this we gained their respect and they would watch us go about our daily business with a certain amount of curiosity. We can now walk right past them and they will stand still then continue eating the communal grass. We respect their *beauty poise power* and *agility* to move quickly and jump over some daunting hurdles (daunting hurdles to us not them).

It wasn't long before the joey was out of the pouch and jumping around with the rest of its family. Then before we knew it there was another tiny head poking out of the pouch checking out the scenery. The mother kangaroo would proudly stand up straight while the joey would observe us from the warmth and comfort of its pouch. This small family of kangaroos would bless us with their presence almost daily.

Whenever we saw the mother we would always look at her pouch because her joey would bring a smile to our lips. We never knew what part of the body would be hanging out. Sometimes there would be a leg, then two legs, or a leg and its head but no matter what it brought plenty of joy into our lives. I was extremely privileged when I saw this little miracle come out of its mother's pouch for the first time as it was unsteady on its feet but managed to jump around its mother then back into the safety of the pouch. I felt very honoured as I eventually saw this little joey permanently leave its mother's pouch to make its way in life.

Howard and I have spent many hours just observing the kangaroos and realising just how family oriented they are. They protect and look out for each other as any human family would or should. Many a morning we would wake up to find kangaroos partaking of the grass outside our bedroom window. Their radar works to perfection because whenever we move they will stare straight at us with their ears turning from one direction to another to pick up sounds. As with many animals it is imperative for their survival that their hearing is razor sharp.

We are extremely fortunate because the woman who built our beautiful home loved her property with a passion so its main features are an abundance of single wood framed windows. Looking out any of our windows there is a scene that would rival any painter at any level. We live in a small valley so every window has us looking out and up into heaven. The kangaroos have featured in many beautiful and humbling scenes as we have learned to understand them. We would never try to befriend them because that is not our right and they have lived a perfect life without human intervention.

Life went on with us and our family of kangaroos when we noticed the mother had another tiny joey in her pouch. Once again we were privileged to watch this tiny creature grow until it was time for it to mark the earth with its tentative first jumps. This little joey is a real character and like a toddler it loved to have fun. Howard called to me one day as he was watching this joey running around our property playing with its mother. It would jump along our bank then back again then continue in, out and around the trees and back to its mother. It continued doing this for quite a while as the mother was standing patiently waiting for it to run out of steam. Eventually it needed to sustain itself for future escapades so joined the other family members who were having breakfast.

There was another day when I was home on my own and this little kangaroo began to jump around our property at a very fast pace. It would jump around the children of the family, stir them up until they all followed behind it then the parents had no other choice than to follow the leader. As you can probably understand they are truly amazing and we love them so much after observing them in the time we have shared their land.

Well back to last Thursday morning when I looked out of the window and there was the mother and father kangaroo and they were standing tall with their front legs touching each other. Then they brought their heads together then backed away to kick each other with their strong jumping legs. I could see this was not meant to hurt each other but it was tiring for them. Then they would sit for a while and rest then tentatively put their arms on each other's shoulders and bring their heads together.

They continued this ritual for how long I do not know because I was totally mesmerised with what was unfolding before my eyes. The male would grunt while the female stayed silent and in the moment. At some point in my life I read about kangaroos and when they mate they do it with force but what I witnessed was nothing like that whatsoever. The love I felt between male and female was palpable and the way in which they looked and touched each other left me rejoicing in the beauty of the creation of earth and every single being who lives here. Eventually the male jumped away and the mother who was exhausted fell to the ground and stayed there for quite some time.

I know kangaroos can perform this ritual a few times before there is a coming together of the male and female for conception. I was and still am totally humbled and blessed at the same time to have been a witness to this magical experience. They are and always will be very welcome to share in whatever they need from this piece of land we call home. They are a part of our culture or more to the point we are a part of their culture because they have lived here longer than humans. Howard and I quite often spread their messages in many and varied places as bits fall from the soles of our shoes many miles from home.

We realised how little we knew about kangaroos before we moved here but in learning we are in awe of them and their family values. They are no different to you and I because when we are shown respect we give respect. We all come from a place where love is all there is so it is up to humans who have free will to embrace each other and *all* our neighbours. Just imagine how wonderful this earth would be if every human respected themselves then carried this respect through every aspect of their lives. How can we expect humans to respect all of God's creatures when humans don't respect themselves?

ANECDOTE

Do as the kangaroo does
It lives abundance
Nourishment is plentiful
Its hearing is acute
Its eyesight penetrates walls
Its tail holds it strong
Its love of family is unshakable
Its knowing of who *I AM* is *I AM*!

LIGHT AND DARK

LIGHT-IS IT YOUR DNA?

To live a life on earth our spirit leaves the purity of light and love to encounter a vibration of density and darkness. It is understandable why our spirit requires a gestation period of nine months before it is ready to be fully exposed to this vibration.

ABRACADABRA AND I AM ON EARTH?

After playing and having fun in the light any former experience of a life on earth would be well forgotten. My spirit knows the importance of an earth life for it to evolve to a higher level of learning. I came to earth to learn and make choices by using my free will, so I must not lose sight of the fact that I am responsible for myself. I arrive on earth with my spiritual/inner light intact then it is up to me as to how, when and where I access this light. How long will it take me to realise my light can only be accessed through love and truth?

In reality whatever choice I make has little relevance to my inner light as it may be dimmed but never extinguished. Do I choose to walk a tight rope and do a balancing act to keep me swinging like a pendulum between light and dark? Everything I do in life balances on a knife edge so I choose as to whether I fall or not. Some people prefer the safety of seesawing in the grey where they hedge their bets and do nothing.

KEEP YOUR BALANCE

On my tight rope there is no room for maybe, might, could, would or should. If I find myself unbalanced what do I do and where do I go? Do I ask other people questions pertinent to me then expect answers? The choice is always mine to make as to whether I walk the path of light or dark. I must remember whatever path I choose will present me with many obstacles to negotiate before my life is completed. When called upon my light will always guide me in a direction beneficial to my physical, emotional and spiritual growth.

Our light has no boundaries so will shine through any physical obstacles to bring forth truth. Our truth will penetrate the darkest of places for us to manifest our outer from our inner light. We can encourage every person we meet to access their inner light rather than basking in the warmth of ours. In not choosing light you will find yourself confronted by indecision and negativity leading you to very poor decision making.

WHY WOULD WE CHOOSE AN EARTH JOURNEY?

Our predominant reason for this earth journey is to explore so we can learn more of what we don't know. This journey we have agreed to take exposes us to physical and emotional pain beginning from our conception. It is paramount for our growth spiritually, mentally, emotionally and physically to learn from every experience presented to us. We are light and dark but it is how we balance these aspects of ourselves that's imperative to the value we get from our life. We have to know we can trust then believe in every choice we make to enable us to connect with our light so we can understand and heal our dark side.

WHO RULES?

The pain of living a physical life has no rules or regulations but is conducive to when and how we learn. When pain is present we must be aware of our responsibility for manifesting it. When we are in touch with our inner self we allow our light to shine then guide us through decisions we need to make to incorporate our spiritual, emotional and physical to march under one banner. When this is our reality there will be no need for rules and regulations because we will be living from our truth and light.

SINK OR SWIM?

Just because we come into this world as a baby does not mean we are exonerated from pain as it comes with the territory. It's us being thrown in the water at the deep end to choose whether we sink or swim. We call the shots in our life as no one else can because they are too busy calling their own. Many people prefer others to call their shots so they can say *it was her/him or maybe them who told me to do it.* There can never be a him, her or them because it is my responsibility to either sink or swim.

When choosing to live a life on earth our awareness goes from the sublime to something substantially lower. The spiritual body knows our physical will need some prodding and probing to remember how to access this awareness. With awareness we experience everything in the moment so its imperative for us to hold onto this knowing so we can live a fulfilling life. Everything in life has two sides so only I can and will ever be responsible for every decision I make.

WHAT IS YOUR DEFINITION OF SURVIVAL?

We know we want to survive so we have to come up with strategies to accommodate our basic needs. When we are a baby we learn that smiling brings approval. When we make noises our parents associate favourably with they get excited and start making noises back to us. We begin to manipulate people and situations for attention when we have to slot ourselves into a pecking order be it family or society as a whole. Through this we learn how to appease our competitive instincts by whatever means we can for our survival.

While we are devising strategies for our survival we can easily get side tracked from our purpose for being here. We no doubt will find ourselves caught up in various games but we must allow our spiritual to guide our physical. This can only become a reality when we acknowledge our physical will never take precedence over our spiritual as they are equal.

WHERE'S MY ARM CHAIR DARLING

How easy is it for me to get caught up in the mundane? How then do I create a life with substance and purpose to take me to the next step on my journey? How many people exist as opposed living when it takes effort to live? How many people stay in their comfortable arm chair then judge others unfavourably who dare to leave theirs? So I have to be prepared to get rid of my well worn arm chair then purchase one that continues changing its position and shape for me to not get too comfortable.

COINCIDENCE OR SYNCRONICITY?

Once again I have the radio turned on as I am writing this story and the song that's playing now is: *ALL MY LIFE IS CIRCLES by THE NEW SEEKERS*.

I will never cease to be amazed by the messages that keep presenting themselves to me. I know how easy it is for our lives to get caught up in circles, then more circles, forming a cycle so we then keep cycling in circles. It's difficult to break away from our circles/cycles because they go to the core of our being. At these times we can veer off course so take stock of where you are and keep pedaling.

DO YOU KNOW WHERE YOUR LIFE IS HEADING?

Would you allow yourself to drift in a boat on a river before bothering to ask how to steer the thing? Do you know how to avoid obstacles ready and waiting to rip holes in your boat while you are in it? Will you allow your boat to dictate your journey or do you take charge and steer it yourself? What knowledge and skills do you require to maneuver and keep your boat afloat? Do your instincts tell you to pick up the oars and row your boat with or against the current? These questions need to be asked then answered by and for yourself, if not you will find yourself steering off your allotted course. If your course becomes easier to negotiate you need to stop and take stock of where you are and make certain you are on your course and not encroaching on someone else's.

WHERE IS THAT CONFOUNDED LIGHT SWITCH?

For our learning we must recognise our light within then speak our truth from our light. The light can get buried under layers of gunk we have picked up on our journey. This occurs when our focus is on survival and not living our truth. It is important for us to keep in touch with the needs of our inner self. When we go within for answers our light will always guide us with love to our place of learning. We will never have to search for our light switch again as it will always be on.

DARK – THE REALITY

Once on earth we have to deal with a reality other than the one we have come from. It is like being outside in bright sunshine then entering a dark room. We try to focus on a certain object in a room but have no idea of what it looks like or even if it is in this particular room. We may be looking directly at it but we cannot see. We will find ourselves taking slow steps while feeling our way around until we know what it is we are looking for.

Somewhere deep within, we know our reason for being here but the answers seem to keep evading us. Every turn we take presents one dilemma after another due to rules and regulations we are told we have to abide by. We learn to create boundaries because if we don't we can lose ourselves in a sea of confusion. Confusion can lead us down the dark and lonely path that holds us in our own prison. Once on the path of darkness some very confronting and lonely decisions have to be made and adhered to for us to walk the path of light.

HIS/HERS, THEIRS OR MY RELIGION?

Many of us find ourselves ensconced in one of many religions who will tell us our answers come from books. We have to adhere to rules man has created rather than our inner voice. We are encouraged to listen to anyone other than ourselves. We face the dilemma of embracing our personal truth or suffocate by listening and believing in the truth of others. We have to see ourselves with total honesty and not because we want to rebel. Rebelling for the sake of being different only antagonises to lead us on a path that's not conducive to us living our light.

Many religions use fear as weapons by saying you will go to hell if you don't abide by our teachings. I was bemused when I realised religions were run by people who were just like me looking for the same answers as I was. They were of the premise they knew the answers but they never did and still don't. They may have their answers but they do not have our answers as we have to come up with our own. It is not our responsibility to walk someone else's talk; it is our responsibility to walk our inner talk.

WHO DO WE GIVE OUR POWER TO AND WHY?

People who see themselves in leadership roles can be big on self so their hunger for power and control will have no boundaries. Leaders of governments, religions or corporations in any medium or media have their own agendas where truth takes a back seat. When we are not living our own truth we are open to being manipulated. This is premised on the fear factor by generating more of the same. By keeping every person fearful you hold the power whereas feed them positives and they hold their own power.

Our leaders deem we need to be controlled with whatever means it takes. When are we going to turn around and say, *enough is enough*! We have had enough of your lies, deceit and whatever else you have used to control us. The mushrooms are heading towards the light where we may wilt but will never lay down and die. A real leader will never take ownership of anything other than him/herself.

WHO'S ANGRY?

Many people are angry and have a need to release this anger. These people will blame anyone and everyone but themselves when they don't know how to deal with their anger. Where do they direct their anger? Inside or outside of themselves? People are totally responsible for dealing with their emotions and actions of and for themselves. There is negativity everywhere you turn. News headlines scream negativity because this keeps people in fear. Fear is a virus in society that holds people to ransom within themselves. This fear can only be dealt with within to bring us to a more harmonious way of living. Really it is only when you deal with your fears that you can live. It takes courage to deal with what is yours and in doing so the rewards are infinite.

WELCOME YOURSELF INTO YOUR LIFE!

I need to ask myself what I gain by holding me in the dark because for me to bring light into my life I have to change my attitude and outlook. I have to be prepared to work very hard to appreciate the endless rewards ready and waiting for me. I have to pull myself out of my self-made swamp, brush off any residue of the old and walk with sure and steady steps into the light. I must allow my light and truth to guide me so I will never walk away from me. I have to stop and take a steadying breath then move forward at a pace I feel comfortable with.

ONE FOR ALL AND ALL FOR ONE

If I fall along the way it does not mean I have failed, it means I have a greater understanding of myself. Many people come and go from our lives as our journey is a solitary one. I have much to learn especially when I come to the realisation that only I can walk my path. People will join me at different times but no one will walk with me from beginning to end.

Allow your light to touch many along the way but never stop moving forward. You will never leave the dark while you are in denial of your light self. When you prioritise your life with material things you will never find true and lasting happiness. You will always be looking for more to fill the hole where your light should be taking precedence over dark.

When we allow our fears to take on a life of their own they will control our behaviour towards others and ourselves. We have to give our inner light permission to illuminate the darkness in our lives so we are able to walk our path of truth and love. Unless this is your reality you will never understand the true meaning of fulfillment. You have to look for nothing outside of yourself to give your life purpose. You have to be there for yourself because if you are not who will be?

CONCLUSION

DARK WILL NEVER EXTINGUISH LIGHT
UNLESS WE GIVE IT PERMISSION TO DO SO.
WHEN OUR LIGHT IS SHINING IT WILL NOT
BE HOLDING DARKNESS AT BAY.
OUR LIGHT WILL SHINE IN THE
DARKEST OF CORNERS
FOR US TO KNOW WE ARE CONTRIBUTING TO A
LIGHTER AND BRIGHTER HUMANE WORLD!

ROSE AND THE THORN

WHY DOES A FLOWER SO PERFECT HAVE
THE PROTECTION OF A THORN?

GOD gave us the most perfect flower that adorns
All gardens in the Higher Realms without thorns
The vibration of the variation of color
Would adorn the most royal of parlor
In the gardens of the highest
How could there be bias?
The thorns signify its protection on earth
So from the higher there is no mirth
With the birth of a new bloom the heavens erupt
But on earth we deem someone to be corrupt
Its sweet essence permeates the night with its secrets
When morning emerges there are no regrets
The rose is perfect in its form
In its individuality there is no norm
The blooms are glorious in array
With perfection comes no spray
The true essence of perfection is still to unfold
The reasoning for their thorns on earth is twofold
We know they must be given the greatest respect
For on earth with fervor we must perfect
The beauty of the rose is for all to share
On earth our challenge is to care
Our instincts on earth are to sabotage
We say this is how we camouflage
Although the bloom is revered in our palace
The thorn is representative of our malice
The earth is all for one
Heaven is one for all
When we know we will die
When we die we will know
The true essence of
THE ROSE AND THE THORN!

A CLONE

A clone is a duplicate of another person or object.

IS CLONING NATURAL?

A clone (human) would have to be produced in a controlled and sterile environment with meticulous precision to reach its objective. I see cloning being more about the ego than respect for nature and its natural evolution. Nature has and will always take care of itself but humans aren't satisfied so will always be looking for ways to interfere and change anything they can.

We are told cloning has its place but we are only told what we are meant to hear. My understanding of a clone is not necessarily conducive to the work carried out in a laboratory. Until we all live from our individual truth we will be a clone of someone or parts of many someone's.

The basic needs of people have not changed but the way in which we go about fulfilling these needs have. The most basic need of all is to be *loved* but not everyone has an awareness of this. People who don't have love in their lives are people riddled with negatives they transfer to others so their load will be lighter. The people who carry a heavy load (perceived or otherwise) deem someone other than themselves responsible.

WHO CARRIES THE BANNER OF REVENGE?

Revenge for what? What do we perceive revenge to be? Do we seek revenge when we believe someone has done the wrong thing by us? Revenge has many faces so accordingly the knowing can only come from any person who needs to avenge and satisfy their needs. People can be precious with themselves then unknowingly create power struggles within.

Respect is a word bandied around with little meaning attached. We can find lies and deceit sitting in the chair allocated for respect. Respect is identifying and acknowledging every individual for their uniqueness. How can we ever respect another when we do not respect and love ourselves?

We all have to go within and ask ourselves what do I want most in my life? Who is the most important person in my life? Only when I answer me will I know the meaning of love and respect because when I love and respect me, I will love and respect you.

DO NUMBERS IDENTIFY ME?

Organisations, be they government or private use numbers to identify each and every one of us. We can then find ourselves carrying around many combinations of numbers as proof of our identity.

Much confusion is created when mistakes are made and numbers are duplicated or mixed up. The onus is then on me the individual to prove to you who I am. This contributes to a society where no one wants to take responsibility for human errors. The computer is always a good scapegoat when humans will not take responsibility for their own mix-ups.

WHO AM I?

From my perspective when people duplicate a person's clothes, mannerisms and so on this is a form of cloning. People play many and varied games while trying to pretend to know who they are. It is so easy to lose yourself while trying to emulate someone else. We seem to have an innate fear of being ridiculed due to the fact that we may appear to be *different*. How can anyone know who *I am* when they don't know who they are.

FASHION CLONES?

Cloning has many disguises and one very obvious example is fashion. How many people keep up with the latest fashions? There are fashions relating to what we wear our hairstyles and so on. When we *follow fashions* we lose sight of our individuality.

Many people who religiously follow fashion believe they are free-thinking and liberated. The joke is on them because in reality they are being controlled by their lack of individuality. God created sheep for following, so the job was never ours to take on but somewhere along the line we have chosen to.

WHAT IS THE DEFINATION OF "NORMAL"?

I know I have had the finger pointed at me many times because I am different. I am told that I do not fit in with *normal people*. I don't do this to be different I do it because I am me. Howard being a mind person likes to pigeon hole people so that he can have clarity on his definition of normal. He sees me as not being normal so I am classified as different or out there. My only understanding of normality is the *normal wash* cycle on a washing machine.

IS NORMAL BUILT ON FALSENESS AND ILLUSION?

Many negatives raise their ugly heads when people perceive themselves to be normal. Comparisons are made and the claws come out for *jealousy envy bitterness malice sabotage* and other negatives to make a cameo appearance. If people could only see the falseness and illusions their beliefs are built on they might make a conscious decision to believe in themselves rather than handing their power over to others.

GET ON WITH YOUR OWN LIFE!

If everyone *got on* with their own life and nurtured their own unique gifts everybody's life would be so much happier. People would not be looking into other people's lives and wanting what is not theirs. It's wonderful to appreciate other people and their gifts but it's not our duty to duplicate them. Nobody is more or less important than anyone else, we are just different.

ARE YOU LIKE YOUR ROLE MODELS?

In families cloning can be a subliminal process observed by others. Many people say *I am not going to be like my mother* or *I am not going to be like my father* when their behaviour tells a very different story. How can people not be like their parents when they are their role models? What do you change to be different? What patterns do you have to change? How do you know what to change?

One certainty is words do not change anything. I know because many times during my growing years I said I would not be like my mother. And yes I was very much like her. One day I became aware I was acting out the same punishment on my children as my mother did to me. At that moment I realised my words had not changed a thing. It was certainly a wakeup call for me to change a pattern I had taken on.

I am not saying my mother was a bad person as she was also flying by the seat of her pants where motherhood was concerned. She was guided by her instincts and need to control her children's behaviour for us to grow into responsible adults.

My mother's life certainly had not been easy with her father going away to war when she was young and her mother having to raise her in very harsh conditions. She was an only child until she was fifteen years old when her parents presented her with a brother. Due to her being an only child in the formative years of her life she was adamant that she wanted to have many babies and so she did.

ME LEARNING ABOUT ME

I knew I wanted love and happiness in my life but I did not know how to go about achieving this. My first marriage was a huge learning experience. I have since realised how adept I was at sabotaging everything I thought I wanted. I loved my husband then my children but it was not with *Unconditional Love*. I still had a great deal to learn through life's experiences before I understood and felt Unconditional Love.

My eldest daughter was only two and half years younger than my youngest sister. I believed I should have had all the answers relating to motherhood but this was a far cry from my reality. For me motherhood was supposed to be an extension of what I knew through being the eldest of eleven children but this was not the case. It was the beginning of me learning about me.

WAS I EFFICIENT?

My mother was extremely efficient in having her housework done early in the morning. On days when she did her shopping or went visiting she would have clothes on the line housework completed and dinner organised before she left the house. All this information was factored into my subconscious for future use (in other words I would become a clone of my mother).

MY EXPECTATIONS OF ME

My mother was my role model so I took on her habits. I had great expectations of myself even though at the time I only had one child. I tried to fit into my mother's mould as closely as I could. I felt at times I was competing against my mother to prove I was as organised and as efficient as she was.

I came to realise I was only fooling myself because no one else cared. I jumped through many hoops before I recognised myself and acknowledged my gifts. I came to realise I never was or ever would be as efficient and organised as my mother and that was okay.

I began to realise this ideal I was carrying around didn't work for me. Somewhere deep within I knew there had to be more but at the time I had no idea of how to access whatever it was. The me that had never seen the light of day but was craving to. I was sick and tired of hiding in the closet pretending I knew me. I realised I was only bits and pieces of other people in taking their ideas and words then deluding myself into believing they were mine.

When I was a child I was not encouraged to have friends at home because mum's routine would be disrupted. I took many of my mother's insecurities and turned them into my own. I apportion no blame to anyone for anything associated with my life because I chose the people who would teach me the lessons I needed to learn.

IS OUT OF SIGHT, OUT OF MIND?

When I look at the females in my immediate family I can see the different aspects of my mother in each and every one of them. One sister said she was going to be different to our mother (role model). Her way of achieving this was to get as far away from the family as possible because *out of sight is out of mind*. Physically this may work but the subconscious never forgets.

WE ARE TEACHERS IN MORE WAYS THAN ONE!

It's easy to follow in the footsteps of a role model because then we give ourselves permission to blame others for us lacking the courage to be an individual. It is all just so familiar so why would we want to change anything.

In my now understanding I know we are here to be ourselves and not a clone of anyone. Our parents are here to teach us what we need to learn.

HOW HARD WERE THE OLD DAYS?

How many children have heard their parents say, *in my day everything was so hard. We had to go without we had to work hard and you have it so easy.* How do they know? They can only speak from their own perspective. The adult can go back to the feeling and pictures they have retained in their mind of the tough times they lived through. How can an adult possibly expect a child to understand any of this? The child does not have any pictures or feelings of what the adult is talking about.

The child knows it's being told how lucky it is to have an easy life. Why do adults want children to have life as tough as their life was? How do they know this child has got it so easy? The child only knows what is happening in the now so why is it being bombarded with all this irrelevant information. We only have this moment as the past is gone and the future is out there somewhere.

DOES HISTORY REPEAT ITSELF?

How many women marry men who resemble their father?
How many men marry women who resemble their mother?
How many people come from an abusive upbringing
then repeat the same in their life?
How many people have an alcoholic parent then have a
relationship with an alcoholic or turn to alcohol themselves?
If there is only one thing I have learnt in my life and that is to *never say never*!
Every time I have said *never* it has always come back to bite me. I am still trying to work out whether I am obtuse a slow learner or just plain stubborn.

How can there be a future when we are not putting all our energy into *now*? What happens when our old belief patterns and conditioning do not work for us anymore? Do we keep delving into the past to give us the answers? We must ask ourself, what do I want my future to be? Do I want the same old patterns I know have not worked, or do I change?

NOBODY OUTSIDE OF YOURSELF IS STOPPING YOU
NOBODY HAS THE POWER TO STOP YOU
ONLY YOU CAN STOP YOU!
The past is a myth the future is a dream and reality is now!

WHO WANTS TO CLIMB MT. EVEREST?

I never wanted my children to experience the things I experienced in my childhood. I must admit with the role took on things were looking ominous for quite some time. I had many mountains to climb before I began to create a different reality. I had to change my patterns and conditioning which at times could be likened to climbing Mt. Everest in sand shoes.

WE ARE TO BE A CLONE OF NO ONE!

Why do people keep repeating the same old patterns? Is it because they know these old patterns intimately particularly when it comes to their relationships with other people? Why do people keep bringing the same type of person into their lives? They keep repeating (cloning) the same old worn out patterns. They have obviously seen these same old patterns played out before and know they do not work but they keep insisting on repeating them. *WHY*?

PULL YOUR FRAGMENTED SELF TOGETHER!

Why would someone go from one abusive situation to another? Is it because this is all they believe they deserve? How far into the abyss are they prepared to go before they try to find then bring the fragments of themselves together? The result of bringing the fragments together will be a beautiful individual living their life through the truth of themselves. This path is long lonely and pot-holed with no short cuts.

It is important for us to know we are an individual and so we must deal with any situation we find ourselves in. We are responsible for our own destiny and no one can control us unless we give them permission to.

THE POWER OF FREE WILL IS OUR POWER TO CHOOSE FOR OURSELVES AND NOT OTHERS TO CHOOSE FOR US!

It is like the delusional alcoholic who every time they have a drink believes this time they will get the better of the drink. Then ten years down the track the same words are being uttered. The alcoholic is in a no win situation so may as well be playing a game of Russian roulette. The only difference is it takes longer for alcohol to kill than it does a bullet.

KNOW WHEN TO MOVE AND WHEN TO SIT?

We may intimately know our family and friends but we have to realise they are only in our life to teach us. We are not responsible for any one of them as they are not responsible for us. If need be put everything that happens to you under a microscope and study it until you know.

DRIVE YOUR OWN VEHICLE!

There are no excuses for saying you do not know or understand because you are driving your own vehicle. You have to choose whether you drive your vehicle from the passenger seat or the driver's seat.

Only when you drive your vehicle your way can you become a whole person in body, mind and spirit. So what if it takes you longer than you anticipated? There will be many deterrents along the way but they cannot cause you to change direction unless you choose to.

Be responsible because everything you need is at your fingertips so long as you remember to look. Don't ever be afraid of asking for directions from others. You can have your cake and eat it but you must trust yourself. Seek then find within the answers to every question you have.

WALK YOUR STEPS IN YOUR SHOES!

You need to understand the reality of being a clone because only when you do this will you be your own person. You cannot walk in anyone else's shoes, so don't even try to. Whatever works for someone else doesn't necessarily work for you. Live your life your way and rejoice in the beautiful person you are!

You will then know the meaning of:

TRUE HAPPINESS OF AND FOR YOURSELF

AFFIRMATION

CHOOSE THEN WEAR YOUR OWN HAT
THEN SHOW OTHERS RESPECT
BY ALLOWING THEM TO
CHOOSE AND WEAR THEIR OWN HAT

IT'S TIME

I twist and then I turn
So now it is time to adjourn
Otherwise confusion will be my best friend
And for this I will have to amend
For the rights and wrongs I have perceived
Takes me to a place where I bleed
I bleed for a life without need
I bleed for love denied
For the only love denied is self love
Self love is a journey that caresses
Caresses every fibre of my being
This unleashes my camouflaged fears
To prod and probe until I change gears
Then the monotone of the ordinary
Will induce me to live the extraordinary.

THE HUMBLE MOUSTACHE

How many wonders can be attributed to the timeless moustache?
My first response is a mouse tache
A place where food is stored for a mouse deprived
What recompense does one expect for such an abode?
There is the moustache that tangles and twirls in an ungainly way
I know not what this moustache wishes to say
Then there is the moustache that curls and swirls
There is no doubt all will be divulged as it unfurls
I know of a moustache grown to camouflage the length of a nose
I have been told it is not my business to know so I can only suppose
What about a moustache resembling Joseph's coat of many colors?
It has often been discussed in many parlors
Have you seen a moustache that bristles when not being heard?
It pokes and prods like a cow when separated from its herd
Then there is the moustache with barely a hair
It tries to intimidate because it lacks any medium of flair
Is it my call to acknowledge a moustache that carelessly covers the mouth?
Is this contrived or maybe derived from the
leftovers of an age old mammoth?
What about the moustache that surreptitiously becomes a beard?
Is this something to be feared?
The pencil thin moustache can leave us in mirth
Is it for real or is it a product of someone who believes they have no worth?
There is the moustache that belongs to one who likes a nip or two
Will this moustache cushion a fall so the owner will not rue
What can I say about the moustache that reaches
into every nook and cranny of the nose?
My lips are sealed because it is not my place to pre-dispose
Then there is the moustache that has the allure of secrets untold
For this I must submit and bring out my blindfold
I have witnessed a moustache that is willing to coerce and traverse
My luck is a fact as I have not been relegated to the back of a hearse
There is the moustache primed and trimmed
then deemed to be sophisticated

It pries and prods while taking pride in its ability to be highly rated
Where is the moustache that speaks only of the good old days?
It sits wickedly hiding its secrets in the middle of its maze
What about the moustache that holds on tightly to its facade?
This moustache holds as tightly to its facade as a poker
player who sits in wait for that elusive card
Who has seen the moustache that stands out in a crowd?
I am sure the bearer is undeniably proud
Where fits the moustache that exudes excessive vanity?
It leaves one pondering on the depth of their sanity
Where must I ask does the ginger moustache come to
its own in accordance with a head of grey hair?
Conversely how can a grey moustache be equated to a head of ginger hair?
Where does reality give permission for anything to resemble a fox's lair?
I am being told to tell someone who may care
A hairless head giving way to a flourishing moustache?
This moustache will snub all in its quest for panache!
What about a moustache that succumbs to the apathy of a carer?
It must long to be introduced to a world that's fairer
We must not forget the moustache that's trimmed
and cared for like a long lost child
This moustache has placed itself in a position where it must not be defiled
Who is responsible for the moustache formed with
the help of a humble but tasty cappuccino?
Our propensity is to avert our eyes and acknowledge our preference for vino
What of the moustache resembling a flesh colored
tablecloth spattered with pepper and salt?
Is it *pepper with salt or salt with pepper?* Whatever
we must not attribute it to a cult
A moustache can only be relative to its wearer
It is not my place to see it any fairer
Mirth combined with truth can be thrown in for good measure
Whatever your preference the timeless moustache
will always be something to treasure.

BE TRUE TO MYSELF

Is truth my reality?
Do I trust in the reality of me?
Where does love fit into my life?
Do I see love as a supplement to my life?
Do I see my life and other people through the eyes of love?
Is my heart open to love?
Are my footsteps light and caring?
Are my words free and sharing?
Are my actions the truth of my words?
Are my thoughts pure?
Do my words represent my pure thoughts?
Do I know the power of my thoughts?
Do I know the damage ignorance causes?
Can I acknowledge the damage ignorance causes others?
Do I know ignorance is no excuse for anything?
Do I know I have free will to choose for myself?
Have I ever taken responsibility for me?
Am I in the habit of blaming every person but myself for myself?
Do I bathe in love and light?
Do I join your love and light with my love and light?
Am I a yes person who suffers in silence?
Does my confidence take a battering every time I say yes when I
mean no?
Does my self esteem desert me?
Am I continually piecing my life back together?
Do I look in a mirror and love the person I see?
Do I acknowledge that I am a beautiful person?
Do I know that if I don't see myself as beautiful I don't know?
what beauty is?
How well do I fit into my perception of living?
Have I ever felt Unconditional Love?
Do I know I am the only person who can restrict me of giving and
receiving Unconditional Love?
Answer these questions with integrity because if not the only
person I am fooling is *ME!*

ADDICTIONS

What is an addiction?

I see an addiction as a repetitive behavioral problem. No one but the person who is addicted will ever know the full impact it has on their life. In many instances the person who is addicted either doesn't know or understand what their addiction is creating.

There are many triggers to manifest an addiction. The basis will often stem from infancy or early childhood. I say this because experiences from our early years are embedded in our subconscious. As we grow *physically emotionally mentally* and *spiritually* a word event or a memory will trigger something in the self that will (as we see it) without rhyme or reason catapult us into an addiction.

There are as many reasons for an addiction as there are people suffering from one. Whatever the reason or reasons; the ability to *live* a full life is diminished. Anyone who lives with an addiction and believes they are living their life to the fullest are fooling themselves. I know because I did.

THE STIGMA OF LABELS

Labels condemning a person of being addicted to any substance or repetitive behaviour is understandable to people who are not addicted. I often hear *normal* people throwing aspersions at people who are addicted without understanding the underlying cause. There is no way an addict could foresee any consequence of something harmless plummeting them headlong into an addiction.

There are also people who have an addictive personality so will seek out whatever they perceive they need. I was one of these people because there was a hole inside that I didn't know how to fill. The problem was I didn't fill it with the one thing that would satisfy me and that was *Unconditional Love.*

The list of addictions will keep growing for as long as people are not in control of their own life. I have been addicted to various unrealities then substantiate any related behaviour in my mind. Self preservation has you holding a torch in your hand without the batteries. The torch represents your outer reality and the batteries represent your light.

An addicted person will grasp at anything to tell themselves everything is okay, they are in control. It is easy to tell the self three bongs a day is not harmful. It is easy to tell the self that after a hard day at work then coming home and imbibing in liberal lashings of alcohol is okay. It's easy to say cigarettes help relieve stress as well as alleviating pangs of hunger. You can tell yourself any story you choose but unless your batteries are fully charged and directing your light on you, you will continue to be in the dark.

It really doesn't matter what addiction is controlling a person because the affect will always have you grasping at and for life. The addicted will always believe they are in control of their life and are making real decisions for themselves. Whether they admit the fact or not an addiction will always control the person not vice versa. Addictions have many disguises but the only person you fool is yourself.

DENYING AN ADDICTION

It's easy to say I know what I am doing and I am in control and I can give up whenever I chose. I enjoy it so what is your problem? Famous last words hey! I know because I have traversed this long and lonely path. Denial becomes a way of life for an addicted person as they deny everything. I know because I have been a master of disguises in showing people what I thought they should see instead of the real me.

If I was confronted with problems someone saw in me I would abuse and accuse then walk away with my head held high and never look back. My inability to deal with my addictions and underlying problems took honest, trusting and caring people on a turbulent journey.

Everyone is dispensable when it comes to self-gratification. I didn't trust anyone because I could not trust me so I would do whatever I deemed necessary to save face. There was only one fool in this whole scenario and it took many years of running for me to finally find the courage to confront myself. My story is mine and there are many other people out there who are caught up in this insidious cycle.

ADDICTION A FRIEND?

Initially the addiction pretends it's your friend. The addiction promises so much then delivers nothing but self-loathing, low or no self-esteem and disembodiment from society. There is a cone of silence surrounding family and friends because they do not know how to approach the addicted person with appropriate words. There is much angst because the addicted person is in denial and believes everyone is against them or is jealous of them.

Do I suggest that the person attend AA (Alcoholics Anonymous) or any support group pertaining to the particular addiction? In my case AA was helpful then as time went on it became an addiction on its own. I believed the people who I surrounded myself with understood me. I saw these people as my friends so I had to attend every meeting I possibly could to feed that addiction. Then when this was suggested to me I would dig my heels in and say *mind your own business!*

PLEASE ASK FOR HELP!

It's extremely important for an addicted person to acknowledge they have a problem then seek help. This help can come in various forms and will lead to walking the path of self responsibility. Conversely addictions can only take you on a journey to a hell. This hell is what you create when you put your head in the sand and point your finger at others for you to feel good.

COSTING OF AN ADDICTION

All addictions come at a great cost to family and society. The greatest cost comes to the addicted as they are cheating themselves out of a positive happy and fulfilling life. They are giving their power to fears and insecurities resulting in a life consumed by poor and unfulfilling behaviour. The addicted person tends to travel through life as a victim and never the victor (well this is from their misguided perspective). Anyone who can rid themselves of an addiction knows the feeling of freedom.

ADDICTIONS CREATE FACADES!

Paranoia sets in when others see through the façade the addicted creates. Addicts are very cunning so will hold steadfastly to denial. People begin to understand denial is always on the tip of an addict's tongue as guilt stalks their every move. Any semblance of reality goes out the door and in its place comes *delusion*. Non addicted people are looked upon as fools. There can only be one fool and that's the person who cannot live in a world without being addicted to one of many substances or behaviours. Hallucinations run rampant in a world devoid of personal responsibility.

DEPRESSION WALKING HAND IN HAND WITH ADDICTION!

From my experience depression walks hand in hand with an addiction. There has to be some form of depression for a person to gravitate to an addiction. The depression can be compounded when an addiction has you in its grasp. An addicted person has little or no awareness of this as they only see themselves from within and not the outer picture.

I believed I was acting in an appropriate manner but have since learnt how deluded I was. I was *existing* not *living*. People who cared about me would point out my flaws and I would pass it off as a joke and believe they were deluded. When I now look back I realise how well meaning and caring people were. I believed they were out to get me or show me in a poor light. I now feel so humbled because there were wonderful people who genuinely did care about me.

I did not see myself in the same light as others so I dug deeper into my bag of disguises to prove them wrong. The thing that kept eluding me was my disguises would disintegrate over time so people were left looking at the illusion who was me. Depression also has its own disguises as I found out when I bothered to let go of my self-delusion to realise truth always wins out over dishonesty.

ADDICTIONS ALSO SMOKE!

Smoking exemplifies an addiction. Many people who are addicted to smoking believe it's only about themselves. *I cannot hurt anyone else because this is only about me,* but how wrong this can be. I have known many smokers who have suffered from one illness or another due to their smoking. I have spoken to many smokers over the years and every one of them assured me that their lungs were in perfect health. There was nothing wrong with their coughing or breathing so they gave themselves the thumbs up. I am sure none of these people have or will ever succumb to any number of the smoking related diseases!?

Smoking is a debilitating addiction. When emphysema presents itself a person still cannot find the strength from within to quit. I know some lovely people who pride themselves in having a clean and tidy house then will light up a cigarette in a public place and discard their butts at random. Streets and gutters are certainly common ashtrays amongst the smoking fraternity and I am not out of line saying this because I was one of these addicts for a time in my life.

SECRET ADDICTIONS

How can a person function at their optimum when they are out of balance? There is no balance when you are controlled by an addiction. Many people think they can tuck their addiction away in a secret compartment and live a balanced life but I assure you this is not the case. Initially an addicted person may be able to gloss over their addiction but this does not last too long because there are always tell-tale signs. Many will play games because there is a propensity to fool others while holding onto their secret.

ADDICTIONS SURROUNDED BY GUILT

There is also the guilt factor. Most addictions have a very deep and painful guilt factor that dictates their behaviour due to their fear of being caught out. A fear of being tapped on the shoulder with the words *I know who you are and I know your secret.* In many cases this fear fuels the addiction because the cycle becomes their life.

ARE YOU MISGUIDED AND APATHETIC?

Well who can you trust when no one really knows or understands you? It is certainly a life of illusion and delusion but in reality the only person you delude is yourself as the symptoms are there for all to see. I carried this self-delusion around with me for many years and truly believed I was fooling others but now I realise the joke was certainly on me. A very sad and lonely joke that epitomised the apathetic and misguided person who existed rather than lived a full and meaningful life.

WHAT DO YOU HIDE IN YOUR CLOSET?

The old saying about skeletons being hidden in closets would no doubt be related to addictions/depression. We have all heard about a closet drinker! A closet smoker! A closet dresser! A closet ----------- ? It is all about hiding what we do not want others to see. If the addicted person took the time to realise then understand the underlying fear they would be well on the way to healing. It takes honesty to look into me and realise a poor me attitude can only manifest into a life of *self destruction.*

OBSESSIVE DISORDERS

In my experience eating disorders and fitness addicts do not suffer from guilt because these can be justified. The anomaly connected to these disorders is when a person is out of control they are in reality in control (or at least the mind is). Explanation needed? A person can see their body as revolting, fat and *justifiably* not fitting in with *society's* idea of the perfect ten. Many victims have been ostracised from a perfect world because they are deemed imperfect (or that is how they see things). They have trouble making friends particularly when they enter a perceived body perfect world.

THE PERFECT BODY? IS THERE SUCH A THING?

Body image is important when one enters the world of entertainment and fashion. Competition abounds so a perfect body (whatever that means) is imperative for an individual to fit in with their peers. What would the statistics be in ballet and modelling alone? How many young people resort to an eating disorder to have the perfect body, the perfect look?

As time marches on body image is in our faces constantly. We are inundated with models who are so thin that a meal we may think of as normal would last them a week. What is wrong with a society selling products saying you need to put your life on the line to give us the look we are after?

SUBLIMINAL MESSAGES?

I recently read about a Russian ballerina who was deemed too heavy for the male dancers to lift. This woman looked so tiny and I am sure many others felt the same as I did. Nonetheless her peers still had the audacity to remove her from her position in the dance company.

Were these people so ensconced within their own minute boundaries to have no idea of the messages they send to young females and males who want to make ballet their career? Males as do females succumb to the allure of the bright lights and performing with the perfect body. How many people miss out on parts because they are deemed overweight? Too bad about their talent. If their body is deemed to be *too big,* too bad! That's life! Who cares about an individual who is real with real feelings?

WHO IS ACCOUNTABLE?

What messages do people in the fashion industries send with the anorexic look recognised as normal? How many young people aspire to become models? There's no place for a size twelve or larger in this dog eat dog illusionary world. How many addictions do these people need to succumb to before they can succeed in a society based on ego? I know when I was looking for perfection I noticed many women with a *perfect body* smoked to suppress their appetite.

HEFTY ADDICTION

It's also very interesting to hear about the diets of the *rich and famous.* There are just so many *wonderful* diets out there that have *famous* names attached so why would anyone possibly be overweight? Diets don't work, people do! We have to be realistic when we decide to lose weight. We have to find a balance in everything we do because when we find that balance we don't have to concentrate on creating a superficial me.

How many people experience the feelings happiness can bring every day of their lives? There never has to be a reason for anyone to be happy. For many people happiness comes by drawing attention to themselves to feed their ego rather than feeding their spirit with love. These people then have the audacity to complain about all the attention they are receiving because what they really want is their privacy. This sounds like another addiction to me.

THE FITNESS FANATIC

It takes a lot of work and dedication to become a fitness fanatic as one must be totally dedicated to the self. The allure of a thin and muscular body is surely a sign of perfection? How many hours of torture is endured to attain their perception of perfection? When I am contented with me there will never be a reason for me to punish me.

ARE YOU A CONTENDER FOR SELF-ACCEPTANCE?

Many people who do not stand out in their own right will turn on themselves and punish their body. How fit is fit? Does anybody know? Well there are certainly many people out there who are trying to find out and will continue to do so for self-recognition. This is a way for people to break out of their victim status and become a serious contender for acceptance as a person.

I was talking to a man recently who was previously into martial arts. His training schedule was phenomenal until his body told him in no uncertain way that it was shutting down. His inner voice saw this as a weakness so ridiculed and challenged him at some inappropriate occasions. It is now a number of years later and he still talks about wanting to be fit but the commitment required is eludeding him. Our body carries us through life so listen to it and look after it because once it has had enough there is a long and lonely path waiting.

THE PAIN BARRIER

When becoming a fitness fanatic the most important thing a person can do is break through the pain barrier again and again. The mind loves this exercise because it means it is control of the whole person. The mind controls the physical and emotional. The mind has its idea of what you can look like so will show wonderful pictures of how you will look and feel when you push your body to levels you never thought possible. Too bad about the negatives that created this monster controlling your life and dictating its own perception of how you look. Realistically other people do not care overly much as they are too busy caring for themselves.

HOW MUCH IS ENOUGH?

The disorder of over eating is also a cry for attention. Many people think these problems are only about themselves *but* this is not true. There is a deep-seated fear lurking deep in the subconscious and it doesn't matter what you do, you never seem to be able to fill this hole within. It doesn't matter how much food you consume because the physical can be full to bloated and the emotional will still be starving. Many people who over eat will not even taste the food as their need for fulfillment consumes and devours, but never satisfies.

LOVE HOLDS THE KEY!

When you crave food do you ever ask the heart what its needs are? This is the only place where the true answers are for each and every one of us. The answers do not come from the mind that keeps okaying the fact that we need food or whatever it is we do to find happiness. When the heart is open and happy we are open and happy and the only food required is love.

We must have self love before we can love anyone or anything else. I know every person who suffers from an addiction has their own personal reason/s as to why they are living their life the way they do. I think what people forget is the fact that we all have free will. We all have choices so everything we do and every step we take is from our free will. How far do we walk down a road that's not serving our purpose of knowing inner peace, love and happiness?

CAN I BLAME YOU?

Anyone who blames someone else or a situation with the belief they are not in control is rubbish. When we are born we are given the reins to our own life and our life's direction is our choice. We all have a voice deep within that knows our soul truth so we need to ask this voice and listen to its answer/s. We then have to find the courage to follow our personal advice even if it means changing our life. Many people will not listen to this voice because when you take the time to listen you have to change. You will then know the blue print you are now using is not working.

ARE YOU PERFECT BECAUSE I AM NOT?

Life is perfect but humans are not. The reason we are here is to dislodge and change everything that's not working for us or for the higher good of all. We are here to understand perfection and to lift our vibration instead of living a reality of a superfluous nothing.

Filling ourselves with alcohol, nicotine, food, drugs and any other thing we care to shove into the body is hindering our progress to become the truth of who we really are. There are no excuses!

I have used many excuses and believe it or not, *none has worked*. For me to wake up every morning counting my blessings then to go to bed every night counting even more is way beyond anything I thought would be possible. I am no different to any other person who suffers from an addiction. I am prepared to do whatever is needed to live my life to its fullest. What about you, what are you prepared to do?

Every person can attain this in their own life but only with total honesty and taking responsibility for everything. There is a wonderful up side to this and that's when you take responsibility for creating wonderful things you live a wonderful and fulfilling life.

SO, WALK YOUR TALK AND HAVE FUN!

ANALOGY

AN ADDICTION IS ONLY AN ADDICTION
WHEN WE GIVE IT PERMISSION TO CONTROL US.
DEPRESSION WILL ALWAYS TRY TO CONTROL US
BY MANIFESTING AN ADDICTION.
HEAL DEPRESSION SO ADDICTION WILL
ONLY BE A WORD AND NOT A REALITY.

WHO LIVES UNDER MY BED?

At this moment I lay prostrate on my bed
So whose messages are infiltrating my head?
Is it the devil I know?
Or is it a line I will not tow?
There is a breeze on which messages flow
But within me there is nowhere for them to go
I am discreet so I only adhere to my own truth
You will never find me sitting in your booth!
I probe and antagonise to my peril
To you it would seem I am feral
I abuse to amuse!
This is only a ruse
I may be prone but I will not atone
Invariably I have thrown the first stone
You may cross my path but this can only contribute to your demise
Then I will nonchalantly block out your pitiful cries
On my bed I will never surrender to the hue and cry of any gender
You will never find me on an evening bender
My orders are constant so I will never have a need to follow
In accessing this knowledge I will never wallow
My bounty is within me on this bed
The voice of one tells me this in my head
My solace is in knowing the truth of me
With this knowing I will never flee
In this life I was granted permission for a body to live
In anguish I know from my bed I have nothing more to give
I now have to access courage to move from my bed
So who does live under my bed?
Do I dare look without any dread?
All I can see is that I am living my life in delusion?
My reality is nothing but an illusion!

SUICIDE

Suicide touches many peoples' lives. When a person is stressed and pushed to the max they walk a fine line. It doesn't take much for them to topple over and find solace in suicide. No one can know where any person's mind is. Does a person call out for help before they choose to release themselves from their entrapment in a world they are estranged from? In their befuddled state of mind they feel their inner and outer world closing in on them with no respite from the pain they are enduring.

Pictures grow distort then reshape again and again to cajole without consent to tear away at every vestige they reach a point of no return. Eventually they have no control over any aspect of themselves let alone their lives. They cannot see through the fog of their reality. They are then taken on a ride to a place within removed from a society they have been trying in vain to function in.

FERTILE OR FUTILE?

When a person lets go of the cord that's been holding them in a *normal functioning* world they find themselves free falling into an abyss with a one way ticket firmly grasped in their hand. Somewhere, somehow they decided to put purchase on a ticket with the guarantee that they will be released from their pain.

In their mind space the person gets validation for their decision and they feel at peace. (When someone is in this mind space they exist in a misguided reality. Unless you have been there you will never know.) The person begins to have clarity around their decision so will attempt to tidy up any loose ends. (Not every person who contemplates suicide will go through these processes but many do).

When someone is at their lowest ebb there is nothing, no light and certainly no life buoys to be thrown their way. These individuals are locked away within their own tunnel of darkness. Their decision may seem selfish to the people who have supported and cared deeply for them. This is not factored into the tormented person's thinking or understanding. When a person chooses to take their final steps it is from their pain and not someone else's love and caring.

WHY WOULD SOMEONE CHOOSE SUICIDE OVER LIVING?

The reasons people resort to suicide are as many and varied as there are individuals who walk this path. Every person who suicide's feels they are alone; no one else could possibly understand or help them. A problem that can be dealt with easily for one person can be seen as insurmountable and untenable to another. Any problem no matter how minute only adds another weight to the person's already overloaded shoulders. There will be a cut off point when the shoulders give way and their load has become too heavy.

These people can walk the tight rope for a long and drawn out time before they purchase their one way ticket. Many people innately know that somehow some way they should be able to overcome their problems. Then the voice within tells them not to ask for help as they should be able to work through their own problems. Asking for help shows weakness because you are admitting you are out of control of your life. To them it is more important to save face by hiding problems than admitting to them and reaching out for help. Once a person chooses to remove themselves from their life they have no awareness of the ramifications their decision will have on people around them.

WHO IS THIS PERSON I CALL ME?

Consequences or recriminations from any actions doesn't take roots within a suicidal person's psyche. The person knows what they are contemplating will have little or no effect on anyone other than themselves. This reasoning comes from a place deep within where pain renders them disfunctional. *Self love are words without meaning.*

I DEEM MYSELF, A WASTE OF SPACE!

There is no room for negotiation in this place of pain. By their reasoning any decision they make is for the betterment of all concerned because long gone is their ability to live a life of joy and happiness. They lose touch with who they really are so any chance of healing and rehabilitation is back there somewhere.

There is never a possibility of them being an important cog in someone else's wheel. Anyone who thinks they are making headway in someone else's life by sustaining (what to them is) a nurturing relationship can be left shattered when reality hits.

SIGNS?

What are the signs a person contemplating suicide displays? Who knows when the two individual reasonings do not correlate? Unless you have walked or crawled along this path you can only surmise, you cannot know. No matter how long or hard you try to understand another person from your perspective you inevitably will come to a dead end. You will continuously be confronted with your own reality.

People who ignore the life they have chosen to come back to live will decide they want out! The going is too tough and their need for a way out outweighs any reality of contributing to a world where the easy way out gets the thumbs down. For a desired outcome you have to let go of your expectations so the reality of your bigger picture shows time and again you weave your own web with your expectations.

MY FEARS TELL ME TO LEAVE?

Subconsciously people know there are many paths so why do they willingly walk the path that leads them into the forest where the stench of mould permeates their every cell. We humans through our free will decide whether we walk through the stench and come out the other side or submit and be dictated to by the belief of *its all too tough*. People may go through the motions of accessing their inner light but in reality knows their fate is already sealed. Their sea swallows them up without causing a ripple, or so they think.

WHY?

I once knew a man who lived and died by the sword (so to speak). His lifestyle was one many people dream about because his work was his hobby and vice versa. He travelled extensively and mixed with the who's who of society. He certainly was no snob so had friends from all walks of life. From my perspective he treated everyone with respect and seemed to have it all. *But,* where did the act finish and the real begin? He was a social person; conversely he held his privacy very close to his chest. It would now seem too close because he didn't reach out to others when his life was hanging in the balance.

How many people get bogged down in financial issues and lose sight of what is important?

TOSS OF THE COIN

I had a story related to me recently and it involved a businessman who had a potentially thriving business. He decided he was ready for a well earned break so had another person come in and run the business for a short time. This person set up a structure then ran the business from an almost bulletproof plan. He brought people together who were enthusiastic and ready to move forward so this was their maiden project.

The original businessman re-entered his business and took back the reins with everything set in place and rearing to go. The person who came in and revised the business was no longer required so he decided to go away for four months. After the four months this person tried to contact the businessman but was to learn he was gone and the business was gone. He eventually tracked the businessman down and was informed by him that because of his now attitude he lost his business. He freely admitted the information to be factual and confided he could not be happier and was totally satisfied with the outcome of his action.

This person is now working for someone in a labouring job, so ultimately he found something where he was happy and his responsibilities were minimal. He wanted less stress and more freedom and that's exactly what he got. He achieved within himself what a lot of people are looking for but don't have the courage to change due to their long term beliefs. He traded a life bogged down in stress for a more enriched life knowing he lost nothing and gained freedom. How many people have also created a similar situation in their life for the same outcome?

IS HAPPINESS CREATED FROM MONEY?

How many people have a windfall after years of struggle and *having to go without?* With money comes responsibility so you can conveniently find you have many friends and relations who are in need of a handout or a loan. This can be a real dilemma because you are faced with responsibilities not factored into your wildest dreams. Then how many people end up losing *it all* because there was no instruction book on how to deal with a windfall?

WATERY HURDLES?

How many people have suicided when they found themselves swimming in murky water? Many people see small steps as major hurdles so make the decision to opt out rather than taking whatever is needed to negotiate these hurdles. Inevitably something is missing within themselves but to look outside brings out the inner fear. From my experience the answers within are distorted and outside answers come from well meaning people who do not know.

WHO OR WHAT IS YOUR NEMESIS?

How many of you create your own escape clause to suit your lack of courage to face yourself? You lack courage to face you and your nemesis whatever that may be. When will you realise your only nemesis is yourself! Until this becomes your reality you will pull everything you can out of your bag of tricks to prove to others that you are okay and are on top of things. It's easy to appear sincere but when inner pain is all consuming any decision made is not negotiable.

Why do we believe money, new people or a better job will change our life? Nothing can change unless we choose to change. Our belief in ourselves outweighs any belief we can have in other people. Our fear of change is insurmountable but only when we deem it to be so. We create who we are so if you are not happy *CHANGE* if your life is boring *CHANGE* if nothing in your life is working *CHANGE*. I know when I had no confidence or self esteem I was too stubborn to relinquish my power over my self belief to change.

CLIMB EVERY MOUNTAIN AND LIVE!

There will always be mountains to climb. Do you submit and do nothing or do you take the steps needed to ascend your mountain? You have within you your own flag at the ready to flutter on the summit of your mountain. When you are in denial illusion and delusion are your only friends.

When you begin to ascend your mountain the unattainable will show up in your life. You will find your eyes seeing beauty and your ears hearing sounds once closed off. Your senses will vibrate at a higher level so you will begin to open your heart enabling you to feel love. Then every mountain you negotiate will have you hand in hand with the courage resulting in self worth. This is when you know its okay to slip and slide because you have chosen to avoid the bottomless black hole.

DOES A SILVER SPOON=COMMON SENSE?

You may have been born with a silver spoon in your mouth but that doesn't mean your life is peppered with silver. Your inner world creates your outer and I'm sure there are many scholars who can attest to this reality. You may be seen to be intellectual but this doesn't necessarily mean you are intelligent. Some people ride the wave of intelligence then bottom out when it comes to common sense. So just because you perceive yourself to be unintelligent certainly doesn't mean you lack common sense. Common sense brings with it many gifts and tools to help you traverse your path in life.

Many people say *"I want to win lotto because it will change my life."* I say *"I want to win lotto to enhance my life, only I can change it."*

DISHONESTY

Many people have suicided due to dishonesty relating to finances. What happens when a person invests their life's savings to have a nice little nest egg then find it has been stolen from them through fraudulent means? These people see their life in tatters with all they have worked towards vanishing before their eyes. There is always a way out you just have to be prepared to put your loss aside and trust in yourself. You have to know how resilient you are and you will survive whatever you put your mind to. Everything you perceive as an end is in reality a beginning creating more and more beginnings. It is time to dig deep and show yourself as a survivor. Honesty creates survivors; dishonesty creates greed leading to a loss of identity.

I knew of a financial adviser quite a few years ago who was an upstanding citizen then somewhere along the line things went very wrong. He had dug himself into a hole, then in his mind he had no way of getting out so he put purchase on a one way ticket leaving his family with the mess he created. He was in a position that demanded trust and honesty and he failed other people and more importantly himself to walk a path of responsibility.

SELF DESTRUCTIVE DESTRUCTION

When drugs or alcohol are present any semblance of rationality is non-existent. You become consumed by and for yourself leaving you without any residue of your true self. Irrational promises and prophesies are made. Then as more alcohol is consumed a morbid side usually comes to the fore bringing with it a bottomless pit of self-pity. One will fossick around in their befuddled brain to find a release from turmoil the self created.

Substances can also bring out inner fears translating into some harmful behaviour either to yourself or yourself and others. Dormant anger can strike at any time to hurt people you care about. I know when this happened to me I would ring people and say things to them I would never have said when I was sober. I would blame and accuse then threaten to snuff out my candle. My three attempts at suicide began with one drink and a bucket full of self loathing.

NO WAY OUT

I had a very close friend who I had known for a long time. She was an insecure and controlling person who was very troubled. She was a very caring mother, wife and friend but due to circumstances going back to her childhood her life fell apart.

I vividly remember Howard and I having dinner with her one night when she told us she was now an alcoholic and wanted to die in the not too distant future. She believed she had nothing left to live for as her pain went too deep. In her mind there wasn't a reason to prolong her life so purchased her one way ticket. Ultimately she had made her decision when she was sober so in her mind there was no room for negotiation and she paid a high price as did her family.

A HELPING HAND

Any person contemplating suicide is not capable of making well-informed decisions. The mind is limited and controlled by its own self-pity so rarely gives a rational option. The mind will distort any situation for its own understanding. It has its own guidelines and will never by-pass these because to do so would send it plummeting into the unknown.

How many people are in this situation? How many childhood traumas keep eating away at us until we find ourselves in a place of no return? How far do we allow any traumas to eat away at us before we take steps to deal with them? There is a resolution for everything but you have to be prepared to look and be open to resolve whatever is holding you to ransom. There are people who have a hand ready to extend but you have to see it before you can take hold of it.

WHO IS RESPONSIBLE?

Until people take responsibility for themselves to journey within and deal with their core issues suicide can be the outcome. We have to acknowledge and talk about all that's troubling us and not use any substance as *to make it better*. Otherwise our unresolved issues will lay waiting like a coiled snake ready to strike at any time.

SECRETIVE

Many people contemplating suicide become very cunning and enjoy the game. This gives them a sense of power because they know they have the controls firmly in their grasp. They have a secret and will not divulge it to anyone. There may be hints and innuendoes but nothing concrete. Quite often a person who contemplates suicide is blaming a surrogate for previous wrong doings. I have seen this game played out and all involved suffered.

TRAUMA

How many people throw themselves in front of trucks and trains? I once knew a truck driver who had a woman step into the path of his truck and was killed. He still vividly remembered the incident and was still traumatised. He had trouble functioning in a world where memories kept tormenting him. Unbeknown to him she had previously attempted to bring upon herself the same fate.

How many train drivers are confronted with this situation? People throwing themselves in front of trains or laying on the tracks to be run over. People who put themselves in this position are extremely traumatised. I know this can seem selfish but when someone is in this position consideration for others is definitely not their reality. They don't want to be here so they do whatever is necessary to find a means to an end.

UNINTENTIONAL INTENT

The effects of drugs and alcohol can cause a person to suicide without intent. If they had been sober they may not have lost all sense of self and taken the same action. Rational thinking can become non- existent when external substances are used.

RESPECT

Every situation and decision can be changed because we have the power within us. I have to take responsibility for me because only I can give myself permission to act and react the way I do.

RECIPE FOR LIVING

THERE ARE NO SECRETS TO LIVING
LIVING IS FACING AND DEALING WITH
EVERY CONCEIVABLE OBSTACLE PRESENTED TO US
SO
CLIMB YOUR MOUNTAIN AND SAVOUR LIVING
THEN GIVE YOURSELF THE GIFT OF
A HAPPY HEALTHY AND LOVING LIFE!

DAY AND OR NIGHT?

With the dawning of a new day comes a new beginning
With the fall of night comes anticipation and indecision
Daylight befits the conductor of a classical band
Moonlight is the torch shining while not showing its hand
Daylight trumpets the dawning of today as a rehearsal for tomorrow
Night trumpets the element of surprise closely followed by sorrow
Day is an unknown where nature is concerned
Night is where justice can be pillaged and burned
Day embraces life where rejuvenation is its only course
Night sleeks then divides showing no remorse
Day gives us energy but sadly few immerse
Night sadly gives way to the evils of commerce
Daylight will always lead us to the path we must take
Night-time can be sinister when telling us to partake
Daylight brings forth the visual beauty of nature
Moonlight casts shadows where there should be rapture
Daylight allures us to a vibrancy we need not heed
Night-time lures us into a veneer that breeds greed
Daytime delivers a kaleidoscope of nature's variances
Night delivers a kaleidoscope of nature's nuances
Daytime brings us together with a heart that's whole
Night-time tears apart our body from our soul
Daylight encourages us to toil in our soil
Night tells us we must give way to our spoil
Daylight embraces us all as one
Night tells us this is no fun
Daytime tells us there will never be winners who are boozers
Night will contradict by showing us there are many losers
Daylight is only a reflection of a world we perceive is real
Night-time is a reflection of our perception of a world surreal
Daylight can be one or the other
Night-time is only the other
Daylight will embrace you for being you
Night-time will embrace for not you knowing you!

COMPLEXITIES IN RELATIONSHIPS

If you don't know yourself then how do you know what you want from a relationship, or more importantly, what you can contribute a relationship?

Complexities enter relationships when people don't know or love themselves. Subconsciously they can sabotage *every relationship* with *every person* they become involved with. People tend to put restrictions on relationships because of insecurities. They expect a relationship to bring into their life what they perceive is missing. You cannot expect to get anything from a relationship you don't already have within yourself. You are putting your expectations on another person and this can ultimately lead to disaster.

WHEN DOES EXCITEMENT LEAVE A RELATIONSHIP?

Its inevitable excitement will leave a relationship. Where does this leave the individual? You can meet someone and hit it off then after you get to know each other on a deeper level cracks begin to appear. You begin to look at the other person and realise they are not really what you perceived them to be. So who do you blame? Is it their fault your expectations were not met? Is it your fault their expectations were not met? No one is to blame because you were both looking for someone who would fill in what was missing from both your lives.

You need to take a good hard look at yourself and ask why does every relationship you enter into end the same? In asking this question you have to be prepared for an honest answer. Were you prepared to give your relationship one hundred percent or did you keep some in reserve just in case?

WHO IS TO BLAME?

Do you blame the other person when a relationship crumbles or do you take responsibility for the part you played? You have to look for patterns in your now and former relationships to give you your answers. Only when you look hard and long will you understand the part you have played. You must recognise you are not perfect so do not expect other people to be. Another person cannot and will not fill any gap in yourself because that is your responsibility.

You need to be very aware of role models past and present who have helped form your idea of a relationship. Look at their relationships then at your own and see how much you have been influenced by them. What type of relationship did you have with these people? What type of relationship do you keep creating for yourself? Why do you keep creating the same type of relationship with same type of person?

REMEMBER THE MYSTERY!

Initially relationships are a fantasy created from the mystery of ourselves and the other person. Most relationships begin on an equal footing when we know our baggage is in storage. Then somewhere along the line the baggage finds its way out of storage to presents itself when least expected or wanted. Cracks start to show and the real you comes to the fore. Lo and behold this person you deem to have treated so well has now turned their back on you and once again you are left with yourself and many unanswered questions.

Do the people you bring into your life remind you of someone you would prefer to forget? You have to know you cannot under any circumstances lose your baggage. It with you for life unless you bring each piece out into the open and deal with.

DO WE APPORTION BLAME?

Yes we apportion blame when that person did not care enough to understand me. *They* had an agenda whereas I certainly did not! *They* didn't understand me so would lump all their problems onto me. I had to deal with the ex's co-workers family friends and whoever else was holding them to ransom. I didn't get a chance to put my side across and I can assure you it was far worse than theirs! I have put myself out for this person so many times and now I have had enough. (And yes this same person was saying the same thing about previous relationships).

WHEN DO WE TAKE RESPONSIBILITY FOR OURSELVES?

We are here as students and teachers so when are we going to realise it's important for us to be both. Many of us think we are here only to teach so find every fault we possibly can in other people. Have we forgotten that Universal Law decrees we learn everything we can from every person we come into contact with, if not it is to our detriment? Never blame others for what *you* attract into *your* life.

Why do people keep walking in and out of the same type of relationship when the exterior changes while everything else stays the same. (Its like painting a house without the preparation required for it to last.)

How many people keep recreating patterns of *abuse submission control jealousy* or any other negative not conducive to creating a real and lasting relationship?

WHAT AND WHERE IS LOVE?

Your mind holds onto all it knows to control any situation you place yourself in. When you come out of a bad relationship what do you say? Do you say "I want someone totally different to come into my life"? Do I say I want someone who really cares for me? Please will someone love me unconditionally? How many times do your words proclaim of great changes you are going to make? Do you go out and reinvent yourself?

These words never worked for me and I am sure they haven't worked for you either. Do you move to another place in the hope that you can begin a new life with new people? Do you change jobs and hope you will meet *nicer* people?

How often do you ask yourself just what your problem is? You are the only person who can change you so stop wasting your energy in trying to bring what you think you need into your life. Words have never or will ever change anything unless your words are backed by action.

WHERE DO I FIT INTO THIS?

I certainly wanted something different in a relationship. I wanted someone to love cuddle and care about me. I was looking for someone I could transfer my responsibilities onto. I know there were numerous times I brought my friend and foe sabotage into a relationship. It took me a long to learn the difference between friend and foe.

If you are a *victim bully intimidator interrogator* or *aloof* and believe you do not get involved in unpleasant issues you need to take a long hard and *honest* look at yourself.

My only problem was me taking myself with me. When I started dating Howard I was lucky or probably more to the point he was lucky as we were in different cities so only saw each other at weekends. I had five days to make sure my mask was in place which left me being me during the week. There were many weekends when the mask would slip and at times disappear completely and was not a wonderful experience for either of us.

Howard was certainly more astute than I was intelligent. I thought I was doing a good job of being the presentable me but no he saw right through my facade. I wanted to keep my rose coloured glasses on where he was concerned because he was everything I had ever wanted. He was gentle loving caring and supportive. Why would I have ever wanted to see things differently when I was holding on tight to myself created illusions?

I shattered my own illusions by sabotaging everything I possibly could. I realised I had been doing this for many years in the belief I had it perfected. Howard showed me the only thing I was missing out on was myself. He knew he could move on whenever he chose. Due to his love for me he supported and kept reiterating that I was a much lovelier person than I believed I was.

I began to feel more comfortable with myself, my children, Howard and the world around me due to his unconditional love and support. At the time I still had a long journey ahead of me and because of this I now have a very different mind frame. I take nothing for granted because to get anything I have had to work very hard on myself.

Howard recently said there was something he needed to talk to me about. He said it will be important for your book. I was getting excited thinking something profound was heading my way. I managed to hold myself in check for a couple of days before I asked him what he needed to share with me.

Well when he told me I really wished he hadn't. He told me of his insight as to why our relationship went into another dimension when we worked together. I thought I had been doing really well and had overcome my insecurities associated with us working together. I was obviously slightly off track because he said he noticed how I sabotaged anything good that came to me. He said I would create a drama so I could keep my distance from him.

Was I supposed to be really excited with this revelation? I did what I would usually do and withdrew from the conversation. He placated me with the fact that I have dealt with so much but I still had this around me to deal with. He said when I came to terms with this my writing would be even more insightful.

Well, I then had to run into the closet to find my humble hat and I can assure you it was well hidden. Find it I did, so I placed it firmly on my head to eat my humble pie. Sometimes I don't know why I am so stubborn as I present myself with more traffic to weave my way through. I have accepted it somewhat gracefully and am dealing with it accordingly.

So you can see it is important for us to let go of the parts of ourselves not working. We all want to be happy and the only way this can be our reality is for us to look at and into every aspect of ourselves. No stone can be left unturned otherwise nothing will change.

WHO CARRIES THE BAGGAGE?

You have to ask yourself just what it is you have to change within yourself to attract a different type of person. You cannot expect other people to change when you think they should. You have to know what baggage you are taking into a relationship then take ownership and deal with the it.

It is really exciting when the baggage is unpacked and strewn around for all to see? It then becomes interesting when you start to wear each other's baggage. Oh it's his, no it's hers no there's too much to belong to only one person. When this begins you have to step forward and acknowledge what is yours because if not every relationship will end up with the same result.

The problem is you do not only wear that person's baggage you also wear the baggage of other people he or she had previously associated with. Then they have this same problem with you because no doubt you have been carrying your baggage around for quite some time. It's no fun for anyone when the baggage and insults get hurled around because he/she did/didn't. Then lo and behold anyone who dares to trod on either you or your partners toes as they will be open to criticism from both of you.

RELATIONSHIPS BEGIN WITH THE SELF!

Over time I had many people point out my flaws and in my now position I thank them but at the time I was not so generous. I have changed to the point my rewards far outweigh the effort I put in. I am surrounded by beautiful, positive, caring and sharing people who have taught me a great deal about myself.

Through change I began to believe in myself then acknowledge myself as a capable person. My loneliest times were when I with someone I thought was important and I felt they let me down. I realise I was the only person who had the power to let me down.

There is only one constant relationship all through your life and that's the relationship you have with yourself. The sooner you get that right means the sooner you can have a lasting and nurturing relationship with another person. Get in touch with the real you, the you that wants to experience all the wonderful things life has to offer. Bring all the aspects of yourself together and enjoy your life. Live life to the fullest, love life until you feel you want to burst with excitement then share these wondrous gifts with every person you meet.

Show others just how wonderful this world can be when you are prepared to leave the old patterns behind to move forward through change. Change is easy; holding onto the old is hard.

There can only be one complex relationship and that's the one we have with ourselves. Get that right and every other relationship will fall into place.

OBSERVATION

COMPLEXITIES PLAGUE RELATIONSHIPS
WHEN THEIR FOUNDATION IS NOT BASED ON
SELF KNOWING AND SELF LOVE
INTEGRITY IS INTEGRAL FOR A
RELATIONSHIP WITHOUT COMPLEXITIES

WHISPERINGS OF A TINY FLOWER!

In your thoughts I am not perfect
Although my awareness is only of perfection
I am aware of you!
Are you aware of you?
Are you aware of our combined beauty?
This I am prepared to say is my duty
I have no qualms in offering my hand in friendship
From my limited experience this should leave you without a quip
It's time to close your eyes so you will know
Do you feel me caressing your sorrow?
Trust your inner to acknowledge
My laughter will be my pledge
Lift your vibration to the land of infinite
The place where only *Unconditional Love* will ever survive
Release the old to the graveyard of the never
Never really was and never will be
The choice is mine to make because
Any illusion can only be a reality of my creation
I never was or will be because *I AM!*

FROM CATERPILLAR TO BUTTERFLY

I know I am a caterpillar I know I am a caterpillar!
How do I know this?
How could I possibly know this?
Who told me I am a caterpillar?
All I know is what I know.
I appear to have many legs.
I mean many tiny legs straining to hold my long body up off the ground.
This does not mean I walk very fast because I don't.
I even spotted a snail crawl past me on one occasion.
My jaws must be very strong because I chew some very tough leaves.
I know there is something bigger and better out
there but I am damned if I know what it is.
I feel it but in the state I am in now I do not know.
I seem to slither and dither from one place to another without
any knowledge of there being more to my life than this.
Oh well I suppose I will never know.
With head down and tail up I try to conquer a dank
and mouldy world hidden from sunlight.
Where I am now there is no opening for light to get through.
I am a caterpillar existing from day to day with the eternal
hope of emerging into a world where there is light.
I crawl about my business in the best way I know how.
Lo and behold I am beginning to feel different.
How different I do not know.
I am feeling myself being wrapped and engulfed in
a substance that's frightening but at the same time
offering me friendship mixed with anticipation.
I am frightened but I know I should not be because this is my destiny.
I have been in this place of many changes for what seems like a lifetime
but I know this feeling is only due to my fertile imaginings.
I am now feeling pain, excruciating pain.
I am drowning in a fluid that I need to make
my way through for my survival.

It is time for me to push through any barrier holding
me in a place I want to move away from.
I huff and I puff then I huff and puff some more
and now I can see a filter of light.
Nothing will or can stop me now because I want
to feel and be touched by the light.
I give one more huff and puff then push myself with
every fibre of my being towards the light.
Oh my gosh I have made it.
I feel myself bathing in a light so bright.
My legs have disappeared and I have sprouted wings.
I feel so humbled and at the same time elated by my transformation.
I tentatively flutter my wings and in doing this
I am transported into another world.
It's now time for me to explore my new surroundings.
I flap my wings to then find myself flying.
I look around me and see colors more vibrant than my
fertile imagination could have ever envisaged.
I know I am where I am meant to be at this time in my life.
I sing with the bees then bumble with the bumble bees.
I am flying with the consciousness of one who knows what
it is to amble around a world where there is no light.
My knowing tells me my life in this form will be short.
I know beauty is an inner belief but living every minute of every day is real.
I know I am perfect whether in my caterpillar or my now butterfly state.
I feel, I see, I sense.
I am living my life in this moment because this is all I have!

THE CLOWN

THE MORNING OF THE CLOWNS DEBUT PERFORMANCE!

The clown wakes early the morning of the first performance in front of a live audience. Many, many hours of intense training have been the order of the day for this clown to fulfill a lifetime dream. Great pain has been suffered in body, mind and emotions to arrive at this point in a career that hopefully will span many years and performances. Many hurdles and barriers have been negotiated and overcome to bring this dream of performing to fruition.

The clown wipes red and sore eyes due to a lack of sleep. Fear is trying to sabotage and undermine this clown's ability to produce a flawless performance. Common sense comes to the fore to enable the clown to once again rehearse the routine with a clear mind. Timing is crucial for this clown's act because one slip, one wrong turn or one blink of an eye at the wrong time could destroy a life's work.

THE BACK FLIP IS THE CLOWN'S ACHILLES HEEL.

Memories of the back flip once again rears its ugly head with the intention of undermining the clown's upcoming performance. The clown knows innately how this must be executed but this doesn't stop the trembling infiltrating and endeavoring to paralyse this tiny body. It is a familiar but unwanted feeling. The clown works hard to control body, mind and emotions from succumbing to this fear. The clown begins to chant the usual affirmation,

This fear is only a challenge and I embrace every challenge presented to me.

Eventually the mind quietens and the trembling ceases while a semblance of equilibrium pervades the body.

AM I ABLE TO MOVE FORWARD WITH CLARITY?

The innate knowing of the clown is to move forward with vigor so as not to get stuck in a void. To avoid this premonition of failure becoming a reality the clown has to focus. When the clown is moving forward a river of energy flows through and around its body. With this energy comes peace and tranquility that can only be experienced as there are no adequate words of explanation in the clown's vocabulary to describe this extraordinary feeling.

After a few moments or maybe longer (as time has never been a preoccupation for this clown) the momentum starts to build once again and the focus is on the upcoming performance. At this point the clown allows the mind to take control. The clown is once again facing its feared nemesis that's once again trying to undermine the clown's ability.

The clown can become disorientated when the mind knows it's now time to do a back flip. The clown hears the inner voice saying, i*f you do not execute the maneuver with precision you will destroy not only your performance but also the concentration of the other performers."* An affirmation comes to the fore:

MY BODY IS SEPARATE FROM MY MIND
MY MIND SAYS MAYBE
WHEREAS MY BODY SAYS I CAN
I CAN AND I WILL!

WHERE THE ACT GIVES WAY TO REALITY?

The clown begins to feel the burden of carrying this weight and the body begins to sag with an almost overwhelming responsibility. Confusion is only ever a breath away from the clown as the ability to differentiate between an act/illusion and reality/illusion is not in the clown's understanding or awareness.

KEEP IT SIMPLE?

The clown has clarity around needs and goals because life must be kept as simple as possible. The clown is not overly ambitious but will maneuver and coerce the life force within to intermingle with the outside world. When the river of life is flowing at its optimum doubts then fears confront the clown. The ever present back flip must be executed for the act to continue with the precision it deserves.

To do this the clown must stop, balance then perform a move that's haunted this clown for many years. If not executed correctly the inevitable danger signals will be flicking on and off in full view for all to see (or so it seems to the clown). Ultimately the clown will fall in an ungainly manner and land without a safety net for protection from any pain that will be suffered due to timing being out of sync.

Another affirmation presents itself to the clown:
I WAS I AM AND ALWAYS WILL BE
WHEN MY OUTER LIGHTS ARE TURNED OFF
MY INNER LIGHT WILL ALWAYS SHINE TO SHOW ME THE WAY.

COMPOSURE OR EXPOSURE?

Panic and embarrassment will set in and take control momentarily while composure is being sought. The clown is never too sure where the pain is deepest. Do physical bruises attest to a fall or does it reside in the emotional? The clown will not see outer bruises because a mirror only shows the front not the back so denial is a distinct probability.

WHEN WILL FEAR OF FAILURE END?

The emotional fallout from a poorly executed move can be likened to the fallout from a nuclear explosion as far as the clown is concerned. It is silent but it is potent. What are the tell-tale signs of emotional bruising? Embarrassment resulting from a fall tears at the emotions and threatens to present themselves to the clown with the worst possible scenario *tears.*

The turmoil and churning emotions within will be either the act/illusion or reality/illusion. The clown will be caught up in confusion to the extent it believes the fall was part of the act.

We must never lose sight of the fact a clown is a clown so then denial will certainly set in where the emotions are concerned. One must always save face so the outer face smiles for all to see and the inner face is given permission to cry. When are these tears within given permission to overflow then cleanse and heal the guarded façade?

WHERE DOES SPIRITUAL/HIGHER SELF END AND PHYSICAL BEGIN?

What affect has this out of sync timing have on the clown's spiritual? The clown tends to forget the spiritual is the higher self, never judging or criticising to bring guidance through life's ups and downs.

The person behind the mask of a clown can be revealed then nurtured cared for and accepted with the respect it deserves on completion of the act. The spiritual/higher self is Unconditional Love and so will always pick the clown up to dust off any remnants of debris. The clown can then hold its head high and walk with confident steps in this life's journey. When the clown falls it is not through intent so there is no damage done to the spiritual because nothing will shake rattle or roll Unconditional Love.

WHO POWERS MY MIND?

Last but not least is the mind. Well this is when things get tricky because the mind turns thoughts into reality. So the clown's mind will endeavour to play a game of hide and seek. When the clown seeks and finds what is hidden the mind must surrender and not gloss over any misdemeanor it perceives. The dynamics with which the clown's mind works does not like to be caught out, so will come up with an excuse every time to save face. The clown has not as yet come to this understanding so believes what the mind is saying. The mind accepts excuses then disburses the truth to somewhere out there.

What another affirmation?
MY PHYSICAL EMOTIONAL AND MIND
ARE ONLY AN ASPECT OF ME
MY INNATE ABILITY HAS THE ODDS IN ITS FAVOUR
SO I WILL LISTEN TO MY INNER
WHO KNOWS I AM A WINNER

THE PREPARATION!

It is now time for the clown's facemask to be painted on. This is a time for total concentration where the nerves are completely calm. The clown knows the procedure intimately but still great care must be taken. Time slips by as many colors blend and merge together with strokes and circles so when completed are recognised as the clown's trademark face. The clown takes great comfort as the familiar face comes to life and with it comes a confidence only associated with the performing and not the real self.

The clown gives the face a thumbs up then proceeds to the wardrobe to remove the performance clothes from their allotted place. With finesse and grace the clothes are placed on the body of the clown. The magic of performing begins to penetrate the clown's whole being. So now the decision has to be made on the hair color that will be worn for this momentous occasion. After much deliberation the clown settles on orange. Adrenalin is pumping through the body as the familiarity of the character comes together. The shoes then the gloves are finally in place. There will be no hat tonight because the schedule is tight and there is no room for any mishap caused by a hat falling off, resulting in a catastrophe.

WHAT DOES A MASK, MASK?

There is a confidence around the clown now that was absent before the make-up followed by the clothes, hair, shoes and gloves were applied. The clown's masked protection is now in place and even the fear associated with a back flip is not as daunting as previously envisaged. The clown can now mentally rehearse the same routine without the anguish shrouding the previous experience.

IT'S PERFORMANCE TIME!

AFTER THE PERFORMANCE

The face is sad because this is how the clown feels inside. The magic of performing lasts for such a short time. The hair followed by the gloves, make-up, shoes and lastly the clothes are removed. Then what's left? The euphoria of performing fades fast and all the clown is left with is the self. The self who wants to hide behind a mask to allow the clown to laugh cry scream run jump and be noticed.

WILL THERE BE A TOMORROW?

What does the clown do to find acceptance within *the sad self the depressed self the insecure self the vulnerable and forlorn self?* How does the clown find comfort in these aspects of itself? Does alcohol or some other substance give the same rush of adrenalin as a performance finishing with accolades and cheering? The bright lights and buzz of performing reverberates through the clown's body for quite some time.

RELEVANT OR IRRELEVANT, THE CALL IS YOURS TO MAKE?

Each and every one of us can answer every question we could possibly ask, but how many of us hide behind the mask of a clown? A clown is representative of each and every one of us at some stage in our life's journey. We all use a subterfuge to camouflage our inner vulnerable self. We may choose to eject ourselves from this responsibility but the outcome will always be the same.

What is left of each and every one of us when our mask is removed? Who is the real self and what façade do we show others to be seen to *fit in*? How much of our true-selves do we compromise to show others the self we want them to see? There is a big *BUT in* all of this. If we stay around the same people for too long the mask will slip and reveal the parts of the self we are trying to hide. Do we keep reinventing ourselves for approval and acceptance? Do we really know ourselves or do we keep our secrets hidden?

UNMASKED?

The clown performs without inhibition when masked but how does the same clown perform without the mask?

We all have a secret self within who knows all there is to know about the self. We know we can trust this secret self because the only way our shared secrets can be exposed is through our physical self. Who is going to do this? Who is going to admit to their faults? How many people live their lives in denial then expect others to carry their load when they lack the courage to be honest? If you cannot be honest with yourself then you definitely will not be honest with others.

INNER COURAGE BREEDS OUTER COURAGE

OUTER COURAGE NEEDS DEEP INNER COURAGE TO SURVIVE

EXPOSURE OF OUTER COURAGE ATTESTS TO INNER COURAGE

DOES HONESTY PREVAIL EVERY TIME?

The only way we can move forward as an individual then as a community is through honesty. We have to remove our masks and deal with the layers underneath. It doesn't matter how slowly we progress because no other person has permission to judge any one of us. The honesty with which we face our fears, then work at healing these fears is paramount to our growth as an individual.

Remember it's always darkest before the dawn. Working on the self always comes with a guarantee of, *it never is or will ever be easy* to face and deal with the parts of *the self* causing drama and chaos.

REJECTION AND ITS CONSEQUENCES ARE ONLY CONSEQUENTIAL TO THE INDIVIDUAL!

These dramas began to take shape from our first memory of rejection. We had to create a space in our life where we felt safe and secure. For protection of our sacred space we learnt to use whatever ammunition we could lay our hands on. We prowled and guarded this space to the minutest degree.

THE POWER OF PROTECTION?

Imagine the power we will experience when we use the same power of protection for our truth as we have our secrets. A secret place has an allure to it. Its where all we have and all we are is hidden. This is our own personal treasure chest with the key hidden in secret compartment within us. It's time to bring forth the key to open the treasure chest and take stock of how many treasures have been stacked layer upon layer only to be forgotten about.

WHO AM I? WHO ARE YOU?

The only way we can experience true peace and harmony in our life is to peel off and deal with each layer. Eventually all there will be remaining is your *beautiful truthful and loving self.*

For some unknown reason we humans ensure our journey gives us a rough and bumpy ride. We are unique individuals but this fact can often evade us. We are writing our own book of life as we go. This book will be a gift we present ourselves when we leave the physical to take up residence in the spiritual.

The clown may now step aside because I am here!

AFFIRMATION

I KNOW I SAY IT ALL
BUT ONLY WHEN
I LIVE IT ALL
WILL I BE IT ALL!

SPIRITUAL WARRIOR

A *spiritual warrior* has no ego to feed
A *warrior's* work is for the light
A *warrior* knows when it's time to fight
Definitely not with guns or grenades
Nor with your convened brigades
Only with the love of one so wise
Duly there is no greater prize
The *warrior's* ultimate is truth of the self
This holds within its grasp the meaning of wealth
The deeper within we dig
The less need we have to rig
The truth is we are now ready to share
This comes from the space within where we care
We must in all honesty acknowledge
Our spirit in the physical has no pledge
The physical builds then destroys
The spiritual builds then deploys
The knowledge of the spirit tells us forever
The knowledge of the physical tells us never
Our *spiritual warrior* knows
The reality of our yesterdays and tomorrows
Can only be realised when we live in the now
For my sanity I have to know how
Because we already are it all
We just have to learn to live it all
Every moment of every day!

AUTOPILOT V AWARENESS

Earlier this week we had our internet installed which was a blessing as this piece of equipment has become a necessary part of our lives. The technician who installed the package was very friendly. I asked him how long the job would take and he replied one and a half hours. My dog Yasman was giving me those looks only dogs can give when they want to go for their walk and the human is procrastinating. I asked the technician if it was okay for Yasman and I to go on our walk and he readily agreed.

LIKE MOTHER LIKE DAUGHTER, LIKE FATHER LIKE SON?

When Yasman and I returned the technician and I began a conversation about how people turn out like their parents. He told me he tells these people to look at their parents to know what to expect when they grow older.

Take notice of their health problems and their outlook on life because that's what is in store for you. I went on to say that may be so but anyone can change this way of thinking by focusing on who they want to be and not who they don't. The law of attraction brings to us the things we put our focus on. It's understandable that when we focus on negatives then you create negatives for yourself conversely the same goes for positives. The choice is yours so don't blame others for the negatives in your life because the buck stops with you.

WHO'S RESPONSIBLE FOR WHO?

Hopefully we have the wherewithal to pull the ace out of the pack rather than the joker to initiate positives as opposed to negatives. First and foremost I need to ask myself, *do I want to be happy*? We all say we want to be happy but what do we do about it? How do you go about creating happiness for yourself? Do you blame so and so for causing you misery? Do you believe people do not treat you in the manner you deserve? Who do you believe is responsible for your happiness?

Wayne Dyer (a well known author and speaker) once said each person teaches others how to treat them. I pondered on this for awhile to realise the truth in this statement. When I first meet someone I have never met previously and begin a conversation I observe their words and body language then react to them accordingly. I am now much more aware of conversations with anyone who I either do or don't know. I now realise right through my life I am teaching others how I want to be spoken to and treated.

STILL CHANGING

Once again I knew the importance of me changing me. When I chose to change the things in my life not working I had to know it was a long term commitment. There cannot be a time frame put on change because change begins with my thoughts and they are continuous. I had to be aware every moment of every thought I had and my reaction to it.

AUTOPILOT

Well back to the technician and his remark relating to people he knows who live their life on autopilot. Initially I did not understand exactly what he meant. He said one couple he knows have been married for many years and they get up in the morning and work on autopilot. Meaning she had her chores to do while he had his. There was no need for them to communicate because they both just knew. Neither would know exactly what they were doing they just did it. Then in the afternoon they would get around to talking to each other.

There was also a family friend he mentioned who would iron every morning just to stay in the zone. She would encourage anyone who had ironing to be done to leave it with her. She never thought about what or how she was doing the ironing she would just do it. It was a practice of hers for many years which to him meant she was on autopilot.

WAKE UP

This had me thinking because how many people do we know are living (existing) on autopilot. When I worked full time I was on autopilot. I now realise due to me being on auto pilot I had no awareness of living. I would get out of bed around 5.30am and begin my day. Then I would get in the car with Howard to travel to work without being aware of what I was doing. It was only when we were on our way to work I took myself off autopilot and into the now.

AH NATURE

Howard and I are very blessed because we live in nature and the majority of our travelling time is spent surrounded by nature. There were days when the magic of the sun shone its light and warmth on a carpet of pure white frost. This was a breathtaking sight as animals were still going about their daily business oblivious to their magical surroundings. We have been exposed to many and various nuances of nature and every one of them was uplifting. Due to us having a two hour drive to work and then home again each day our love of nature made it doable. (I am now fortunate because my travelling to work days are over.)

STAY AWARE

Awareness has to be at its optimum on foggy days as visibility is in the now not in front (future) or behind (past). A driver has to be totally aware and in the moment otherwise a catastrophe is waiting in the wings and ready to pounce. There is no room for the complacency of autopilot when awareness is paramount for survival.

We were also challenged with black ice on the road. Awareness was the order of the day for Howard as cars were sliding off the road willy nilly. There were your home grown family cars then there were cars towing trailers as well as vans and an occasional truck. Luckily the trusty tow trucks were parked spasmodically along the road ready and waiting to pick up a job or two.

WHO TO TRUST?

Howard is an extremely competent driver who is aware of his surroundings and conditions at all times. I on the other hand have to work hard at staying aware. Howard began driving from an early age and always respected cars and what they are capable of. He has raced cars as well as having competed in rallying so his awareness is crucial for his as well as other people's survival. His business is predominantly brakes and clutches so he knows the value and importance of stopping a vehicle. He takes total responsibility for every vehicle that leaves his workshop and knows the importance of brakes working at their optimum.

WHO NOT TO TRUST

I have to shamefully admit that at times I frightened myself by allowing me to go on autopilot while driving my car. I found myself having to give me a lecture to stay aware *now*. Part of my job was to deliver and pick up parts so I was on the road for varying amounts of time. I had some very close encounters with other road users so my awareness was surely tested.

At times I would say to myself, *I know am sitting in the driver's seat with my feet on the pedals and my hands on the steering wheel but who's driving?* My awareness was sitting in the passenger seat while my autopilot was driving.

I would blame it on tiredness or boredom but these were excuses not answers. I began to challenge myself constantly to keep myself aware now. This worked because I made myself take notice of the traffic around me as well as the road I was travelling on. This helped me in the many aspects of my life where I could take myself off autopilot and into awareness.

THE INTERNAL VOICE

I have to be aware of my internal voice because it keeps trying to take me to a place of its choosing. This was evident when I tried to meditate. I would clear my mind by focusing on my breath. Then without realising what was happening I found myself making a list of groceries I needed to make the casserole for the night's dinner. Then I would begin to make plans for the weekend. Next I would be on the phone having a conversation to somebody about organising something for what I have no idea. Then I would find myself in the house itemising any housework requiring attention. All this happened while I was sitting in my meditating position and supposedly in the now. Crazy isn't it because that's what meditation is for. It would seem as though my awareness has given way to autopilot many times.

TAKE CHARGE

I have now taken steps to hold myself accountable for every choice I make. No one else can ever make a choice for any of us that we do not agree with because we are the only ones who can choose for ourselves. If I am not happy doing something because I believe I am doing it to make you happy then I am wrong. It's not my job to *make anyone else happy; it is my job to make me happy.*

It really is time for me to dismantle my autopilot and bring my awareness into the now, because without awareness *I will never be in the now!*

STAND UP THE REAL ME

I realise just how fortunate I am to now live in the country. Initially after leaving the burbs I was still on autopilot, I saw but I did not see. I had trouble settling in to my new life as I kept staring my same old negatives in the face rather than looking for positives. I began to work on our property by chopping and stacking wood while clearing away the rubbish as I went. Somehow I never totally embraced it as being a part of me. I would admire the wonderful native life around who brought great joy but there was always something missing.

RELEGATED TO THE PAST

I wanted to spend days on my own but I could never embrace the actuality of what I wanted. When I lived in the burbs I would frequently have my radio tuned in to my favorite talk back radio station. This is now a memory because where we are living there is no signal so my radio listening days are over.

I now have no interest in listening to any radio station because I have found contentment within myself. I now enjoy the solitude of my own company and have opened my heart and mind to my surroundings. The aspects of myself that needed to be occupied have been relegated to the past. Now every day I have an awareness of everything important in my life for me to cherish.

THE BEAUTY OF NATURE

My senses have developed and my awareness has multiplied since I bothered to wake up. Kangaroos and wallabies as well as the kookaburras who herald a new day with their laughter greet me. There are also the water hens and ducks who swim and hunt for food on our lake. There are also the magpies who join as one to create magic with their song. There is also our neighbor's duck that comes to visit of a morning to partake of breakfast and swim in our lake.

There are no weak links in my life now and this is due to my heightened awareness. I feel humble whenever I walk around our property because it has been, is now and always will be, whereas I am but a ship passing in the night.

RETIREMENT

After all that I find I am still talking to the technician with the realisation of how close our autopilot is and the importance of staying aware. He said there were a few men he knew who had retired from their positions then died a short time later. I told him about my father when he was facing imminent retirement and how he devised a schedule that had him doing something every day.

He enjoyed golf but due to work had little time to play so he delegated himself two days a week to swing his club. He also helped out at a charity whenever possible. Then every Friday he would venture to my sister's place in the country to help her with her outside chores. In this way he visited my sister and kept himself physically fit at the same time. He would also go for a long walk every morning to keep himself fit and healthy.

For women it is a different story. Many women have been used to a certain lifestyle and are not open to change. They are not used to having a man around the house during the day. Even when there's no need to get up early their operational autopilot has been working for so long they don't know how or want to turn it off. Certainly this is not the scenario for every person male or female who retires but there are many and varied adjustments needed to be made.

Then there are the people who plan to travel but never do. There are others who travel once or twice a year and are others who travel constantly. No matter what it's important to have plans in place when retirement comes around because there is an autopilot just around the corner waiting to be turned on. Sometimes people do need to dig deep within themselves to set a plan with a touch of flexibility thrown in.

THIS MOMENT IS ALL WE HAVE

For any one of us to live our life to its fullest we have to stay in the moment. The past is exactly that, past and the future is what we create from this moment. It makes no sense at all to regurgitate the past because you cannot change a thing. You can hold yourself in a place not conducive to you being happy in the now. The future can be feared when you're stuck in the past.

How can our body ever move forward when our mind will not? How can our body ever recover from an illness when our mind is living in the past? How can we see the light of day when the dark of night is our reality? How can we ever move forward when we keep sliding backwards? Where is our future when it is steeped in the past? How can we enjoy the beauty life has to offer when our past is controlling our now? What does it take to forgo the autopilot in order to be aware?

Everyone has a past with many and varied experiences and its all they are. Unless you want to stay on autopilot for the greater part of your life dismantle it and be happy. Let go of the past and embrace the now. I know this can be difficult when people are not aware of their inner power to create a fulfilling and joyful life.

LET GO OF YOUR AUTOPILOT TO LIVE WITH AWARENESS

What is easier, walking in the swamp of the past or living in the luxury of now? The experiences in the past can have no relevance to now unless we give them permission to do so. Living your now from your past is not living it is you walking in the steps of what was and will never be. No doubt there are many varied and wonderful experiences in the past and all they can be are -*MEMORIES*-.

It is our duty to live in this moment because this is all we have!

ACKNOWLEDGEMENT

A MOMENT IS BUT A BREATH
SO TAKE A BREATH
AND KNOW THIS IS ALL YOU HAVE
BECAUSE THE PRECIPICE OF TIME
HAS LEFT ITS CALLING CARD WITH
YOUR NAME ENGRAVED ON IT.

INDECISION

I awaken with the residue of sleep in my body
So where is my focus?
Is it in the kaleidoscope of my dreaming?
Is it planning my day ahead?
Is it floating in yesterday?
Is it demanding to be propelled into tomorrow?
Where am I?
What am I thinking?
This is today
Yesterday is but a memory
Tomorrow could be anywhere
*So w*ake up and breathe in the moment
Then my future will be created from *now!*

SUCCESS

I am perplexed with the implications of success.

Success is afforded to every aspect of our lives. As it's not a tangible it can only be measured then justified by an individual from their knowing. Innately our purpose is to be a free thinking individual. Our yardstick for success comes from our guiding influences that includes teachers, parents, religions and society in general.

TRANSLATING SUCCESS

Somewhere along the line many of us lose the true essence of success. Success without the attachment of a demanding ego. My idea of success is to go to sleep at night and wake up in the morning with a smile on my face.

Society creates many yardsticks for success and this is all a part of the illusion. The feeling success gives us eventually wanes leaving us wanting even more. Success can take us on a journey within to places untouched. Success takes us to the highest of high mountains only to throw us into the depths of despair and pain when the euphoria of success evaporates.

HERE TODAY GONE TOMORROW

Gone is the exhilaration we experienced from an achievement. Success can take you to the top of a ladder only to be confronted with unsecured rungs. You then find yourself slipping down the ladder quicker than it took to get there. How does it feel to have invested so much energy in striving for success then reality strikes to dissolve your illusion? How far up the ladder do you need to go before you consider yourself as successful?

GAUGING SUCCESS

How do you gauge success? Our mind is the controlling factor in our life so when we allow it to dictate what success is we can find ourselves on the wrong train. Our mind constantly changes its direction depending on what we are doing at the time. The mind watches and listens to other people either through the media, friends, family or society in general to gauge its idea of success. Then the mind will busily tell you what you should do to become a success.

SUCCESS AND ILLUSION

The mind can be very diligent in its quest to prove how competitive and successful I am. I will show everyone that I can achieve anything I set myself to do. I want to be the biggest and the best and have the biggest and the best so they will know how successful I am.

This is all an illusion! How many rungs does a ladder have? Do people believe success can be measured in a physical body controlled by the mind? True and lasting success comes when we know ourselves from within. Only when we know and live our purpose will we know success.

Success within does not need approval and will definitely not encroach on another person's space. Inner success does not need to steal ideas or feed off anyone's energy. Inner success dances to its own tune because it knows *a pure heart harbours a pure spirit.*

With this knowing comes greater understanding of ourselves and our limitations in dealing with obstacles we encounter in life. Success can be assessed by and how we deal with obstacles then integrate them into our life to nurture our growth, resulting in a more loving and caring me.

RESPONSIBLE OR BLAME

When I come from my truth I will take full responsibility for myself and not apportioning blame to you for my decisions. There can be a tendency to go back to a time when I believed I was badly done by. I will point the stick at you and say you did or did not......... then give myself permission to hurl the blame at you. By doing this I take myself into a victim mode rather than dealing with what I am confronted with on its merits.

TO BE OR NOT TO BE RESPONSIBLE

In childhood we learn the importance of success as being a way to *fit in*. A child will do things to draw attention to themselves without the intent of an adult. An adult draws attention to themselves for self gratification due to insecurities. Success and insecurities do not make very good house mates as I am sure many people have found out.

Adults will always have excuses as to why they are not succeeding in their life. There are any number of excuses on the tip of a person's tongue when a finger is pointed at them for being unsuccessful. This can become a way of life when you chase success because you will then find it chasing you away. *I win, you lose*. In the game of life there are no winners or looses because we are all equal.

When you strive for success you will continually be grasping at straws because there are no limitations on success. Success is only related to the physical and as we know we all have our used by date secured deep within us. The inner self has no need of outside success because it always was, is and will be.

YOU MAY WELL ASK

When adults have not dealt with any childhood issues relating to success or lack of they tend to play games with other people. They have to win at any cost because they equate winning to success. Successful games do not walk hand in hand with success by playing games. Only an unhealthy ego decrees me successful due to beating an opponent. Euphoria through winning is only a puff of smoke, here one moment then gone the next.

SUCCESS AND RESPECT

To be successful as an individual we have to respect others no matter who they are. Society tells us a different story because unless I am successful I will be insignificant in their world. Success has many facades, agendas and innuendos. Success is attributed to *sporting, media, corporations, politicians and so it goes.*

Success is short-lived and will devour you without even remembering who you were and what you were successful at. How many people do you hear about in your life who have been accredited with being successful and then disappear into to the ethers never to be heard of again? How many *successful people* turn to substances because they are no longer recognised as *a successful person*?

Why does the *ordinary street person* feel humble in the presence of a *successful person?* There is a great deal of money to be made when you are a successful person. You demand respect and bathe in the accolades you believe you deserve. Outer success in reality has no meaning when it comes to individual success. I am a success in my life because I love and respect me, so then I love and respect you. It's not because I am an out there successful person, it is because I know the difference between outer and inner success.

CHECK YOUR KIT BAG?

To live life to its optimum *honesty truth respect compassion humility faith joy laughter peace and unconditional love* must be the most used tools in our kit bag. When we live with these tools as our reality our every moment will bring us happiness and contentment.

WHAT IS SUCCESS FOR ME?

Is it passing exams, acquiring the job I always wanted, buying a house or making my way up the corporate ladder? *What is it for me?* There are as many ideas of success as there are people on the earth. How many people's lives are guided by their idea of success? How many people when taking their last breath congratulate themselves on their outer success in life?

Success for me is to live every moment to its optimum. It is staying in the now and not allowing my mind to dash off somewhere whenever it chooses. My mind tends to revisit a conversation I had yesterday then tries to tell me how I should have approached it. I should have said this then that and I surely would have made better decisions. Oh the mind never to stops wandering so we need rein it in and keep it in the now. Any person who can do this is a success.

SUCCESSFUL LADDER CLIMBING OR LADDER OF SUCCESS?

Many people who begin to climb their perceived ladder of success give themselves permission to judge and criticise other people. It is easy for the ego then to step in and recognise then demean others because of their perceived inadequacies, shortcomings and lack of ambition. You need to keep your ideals and ideas to yourself because you still have much to learn firstly about yourself and then other people.

The corporate ladder is certainly a great yardstick for success with back stabbing, griping, nastiness and jealousy envy a total lack of respect the self and others. This is totally out of step with the deeper meaning of success. You will never have any understanding of success if you have to look for it outside of yourself. True success resides within each and everyone of us.

CAN I CREATE MY OWN SUCCESS?

When you look outside yourself for success you drag other people's ideas and beliefs to you then surreptitiously take them on as your own. Success is transient so requires topping up moment by moment. You can create success for your mind but you cannot for your spiritual as you already have it.

WHOSE SUCCESS IS EQUAL TO YOURS?

How many people cannot acknowledge we are all equal? Due to this fact we still like to dither around in the realm of differences rather than acknowledging the beautiful person we all are. With inequality comes separateness resulting in competition. I am better than you! Oh no you're not because I have proof that I am the best and so it goes. This is why people do not live as one because it only takes one individual ego to create chaos among the many.

CORPORATE SUCCESS?

We then move into the corporate sector where we are confronted with another set of guidelines for success. Corporate success mostly relates to how much money they can get out of the *ordinary people*. Its big business because strategies have to be put in place and all the maths done so the corporations cannot lose.

We have our salaries then our investors to consider so we have to be successful no matter what it takes. Success equates to money and money equates to success. How much money can a corporation afford to lose and still be successful? Due to all this stress our remuneration has to be substantial due to all the energy I am putting in. I am making a lot of money for a lot of people so I must be successful.

IS SUCCESS EQUATED TO STATUS OR STATISTICS?

Many people measure success by what school you went to, what job your father had, where you lived or how much money you could earn. How many people relate success to money? Too many! Money breeds *greed segregation control* and a false sense of power.

Is there enough money to buy what is important in life? Definitely not! The most important things in my life have nothing to do with money. I have beautiful, genuine and honest people in my life who I love dearly and I certainly would not be able to recognise these qualities in people if I attributed success to money.

Statistics have many friends but status thinks it has many more!

SUCCESS OR THE ILLUSION OF SUCCESS

I have learned the importance of letting go of the *illusion of success* to be a success. I am and will always be learning about and enjoying the true meaning of success through *Unconditional Love* for myself and others. To live *Unconditional Love* is our only *real* guide for success!

AFFIRMATION

MY INNER SELF IS SUCCESSFUL
SO IT IS TIME MY OUTER SELF REALSISED
IT CANNOT SEPARATE ITSELF FROM
MY INNER SELF
SUCCESSFULLY!

WHY AM I SITTING ON THIS BRANCH?

Who chose this branch?
Who do I please by sitting on this branch?
How will I know if I am pleasing me?
I have to ask myself *"why would I ask such an absurd question?"*
Am I saying I do not know me?
Is it time for me to get to know me?
Fear upon fear is presenting itself to me
Confusion is now intermingling with my fear
So where do I go to find some quiet space?
Ah! I am already here sitting on this branch
How can I possibly stop the chatter infiltrating my head?
With this I close my eyes and begin to sway
I grab and clutch at the unknown
I begin to steady and familiarise myself with the security this branch offers
In my quest to secure myself on this branch I find
the chatter in my head is now dead
I am beginning to feel the breeze as it caresses my body
The rustle of the leaves is reminding me of times gone by
Times when I was a child sitting on this very same branch,
With stars in my eyes and an outlook on life
befitting the innocence of a child
I feel my heart beginning to open like a rose on a beautiful spring day
Memories besiege me as thunder reverberates in a storm
Smells, tastes and feelings are assailing my raw emotions
Remembrances of times gone by or maybe it was only yesterday
As I open my eyes I notice an array of changes taking place
With a jolt I realise the only thing changing is me!
I know this precious branch will be with me wherever I go
My subconscious is telling me it always has, and will be mine
All my yesterdays and tomorrows can only be related to my now reality!

CONNECT OR DISCONNECT

When we were born we came with our own tiny vehicle and a tiny caravan connected to it. It was our duty to drive our way through life to upsize our vehicle while downsizing our caravan. How many people have achieved this?

THE JOURNEY BEGINS

When we began our journey everything was shiny and new and we were moving forward at a steady pace. Then something happened and we began to lose ourselves in things outside of our vehicle and caravan. We were not breezing through life as we were meant to. We seemed to be confronting one obstacle after another until we lost sight of where we were heading. There may have been signposts but we couldn't see them through the fog consuming us.

BUMPS ALONG THE WAY

Then things began to shift and change within ourselves resulting in our vehicle being harder to control. Then the caravan began to have an aversion to sitting snugly behind our vehicle as it was displaying signs of wanting to go in one direction while we were trying to hold it in another. The vehicle became a lot more erratic in its towing capacity because without any indication we would find ourselves veering to the other side of the road.

Then within the blink of an eye did you find yourself facing oncoming traffic? Did you try to take on the oncoming traffic or did you maneuver back to the other side of the road? Did you remonstrate with people around you by telling them you knew exactly what you were doing and if they had a problem to get over it? What strategies did you put in place to never allow it to occur again? Did you take responsibility for yourself or did you point your finger at others?

WHO IS DRIVING YOUR VEHICLE?

Where were your thoughts coming from? Were they yours or were they planted there by people whose agendas did not correlate with yours. How could you come to any conclusion when as it would seem only moments ago you were starting out on your journey in your untarnished vehicle and caravan? Who have you allowed to infiltrate then control you? Who is blocking you from using the indicators in your vehicle to know in what direction you need to travel?

There is also your struggle to keep your steering wheel in your hands while many other hands are trying to unnerve you by taking over the driving of your vehicle. All these people have their own agenda's so they will use whatever it takes to have you a passenger in their vehicle rather than you driving your own. You know you have a lot to learn because you keep getting told you do. You have to learn about life and people to know whether they are good or bad. You have to know when to stop and listen then when to continue without interruptions.

FACE YOUR FEARS

You need to know when to stop your vehicle and take a breather. You have to communicate with, then mix with people but you have to be discerning. You have to face rejection and all the misguided feelings that come with it. You have to know how to deal with everything you are confronted with for your learning. What do you do? Do you open your caravan door and throw your unwanted fears and feelings inside to deal with when you are ready? When this happens do you find more fears throwing themselves in front of you while you are in the process of trying to stabilize your vehicle? How do you face these fears and associated feelings? Do you ride roughshod over them and pretend they were never there or, do you stop to look them in the eye then face them head on?

WHAT WAY IS FORWARD?

When you ride roughshod over your fears and associated feelings do they continue presenting themselves to you in one form or another until you do face, then deal with them appropriately? What other sign posts are you confronted with along your journey? Do you find from time to time people throw things at your vehicle and caravan? Do you then find your caravan swaying from side to side while you are trying to forge your way ahead? Then when things begin to move along smoothly you have a blowout. You lose traction as your vehicle is heading in one direction while your caravan with its blown tyre is threatening to overturn and cause chaos to your wellbeing.

Do you keep persevering or do you stop and sit for a while to take stock of your situation? Do you then give yourself a plan to follow with the intention of sticking to it? Do you tell the rabble within you to keep quiet while you formulate your plans for your future? Do you then tell people of your plans only to find them trying to undermine you? Do people tell you the reason you cannot change is because it takes courage and lashings of self belief? Do you then have the courage to say, *"get out of my vehicle and leave me alone because this is about my life and I will drive to my own tune whether you like it or not"*?

WHERE TO NOW?

What happens when you find yourself on your own once again and feeling very happy with your lot in life? Do you get caught up in your own thoughts and forget about the bigger picture only to be confronted by a precipice? This precipice represents you allowing other people to drive your vehicle without them knowing who you are and what you are here for. Invariably the buck stops with you so if you need to go over the precipice for your learning so be it.

All this time while you have been busy navigating your life have you bothered to check out your vehicle and caravan? Did you think they would take care of themselves? I am by now sure you have found your vehicle and caravan are as clogged up with rubbish as you are.

TLC PLEASE

Your vehicle is now sluggish and your caravan is in much need of some tender loving care. You have not nurtured the most important things in your life. You have been too busy listening to other people and taking on board what they have said rather than listening to and believing in yourself. You have neglected yourself and your needs to sustain you for your life. You have to look at and acknowledge the times you have been in disrepair? Who or what has been driving your vehicle and caravan? Are you moving forward or are you stuck at the crossroads not knowing which way to go?

TIME FOR REPAIRS

Now is the time to stop and take stock of your life. Get out of your vehicle and check out the condition it is in. Does it need a service? Are the brakes worn and squeaking? Are the tyres bald with wire showing through? Is the paint work scratched and peeling? Are the windows chipped and dirty? Check underneath to see what debris has been gathering in places you did not know existed. How much rubbish have you been accumulating in the boot and on the back seat? Can you see out your rear view mirror? Is your caravan in pristine condition? Ask yourself then give an honest answer to each question. Only then will you point your vehicle in the right direction for you.

TIME TO DISCONNECT

During this whole journey have you bothered to look inside your caravan? If not prepare yourself for a shock! Did you at any stage think it would be prudent to disconnect your caravan from your vehicle? Well now is the time! Disconnect the caravan then make your way inside and see just how much of nothing you have accumulated without awareness.

THROW OUT THE OLD

I am sure there are a variety of pungent odors infiltrating your nostrils. I bet at some time someone suggested you stop to smell the roses so you picked one for now and more for later. Seek them out as they will be dead and decaying by now. Then there are all the clothes you kept just in case. Just in case what? Did you use your excess baggage as padding to keep you warm on a chilly night? Nothing you cart around in your caravan can be useful unless it serves your purpose.

Throw out and discard the old then make friends with a lighter and clearer you. Let your light shine on the mouldy and dead that never has or could serve you or your purpose. These unwanted nothings will only hold you in a place where there is no forward movement. You will continue to slip and slide backwards without any awareness of this occurring until you choose to change.

Change is not about regurgitating the old; it is about bringing in and embracing the new! Without you realising it your caravan has expanded to take in the old and useless to leave you with nothing other than a pain in the neck. There no doubt have been many other pains along the journey but now it is time to release them all.

A MAKEOVER PLEASE

It's time to give yourself, your vehicle and caravan a makeover. Do not just do it willy-nilly! Do it with precision because this is all about you and your life and the direction you want to travel. Give yourself the gift of this time to disconnect from all that's holding you in a place where your needs have not been met.

Disconnect from everybody and everything so you will know who you are. Only then will you be in a position to drive your life in your direction without interference. It's time to upsize your vehicle and downsize your caravan. Surprise yourself with a strong and reliable vehicle as well as a caravan that tows perfectly behind your vehicle.

YOU CAN ONLY KNOW YOU

No one else can know you like you know you! Listen to people but be discerning because they are all coming from their own perspective! We are all unique and beautiful but many of us never know it! We have been created from perfection therefore it is up to every individual to acknowledge this fact!

*Humans, due to their free will see only what they
want to see and not the reality of what is!*

KNOWING

KNOW WHEN TO CONNECT
THEN KNOW WHEN TO DISCONNECT
IF YOU MIX THEM UP
YOU WILL BE SITTING AT THE
CROSSROADS IN CONFUSION
TO NEVER KNOW THEN LIVE YOUR PURPOSE!

WHERE IS THE LIGHT? WHERE IS ME?

This hole is so dark and dank
So where is the light?
Has there ever been light?
Am I condemned to this nothingness forever?
My tears are at the ready to show the world my despair
I know there is no one out there who has ever cared
BUT, if someone did care, how would I know?
My only awareness is of pain and despair
I grapple and fumble to find the switch to turn on my light
Then a voice from afar suggests I look within
Surely I have overbalanced and fallen into the abyss
Am I so consumed by misery that I have been blinded to the light?
I feel myself spiraling further and further into the unknown
My head is being infiltrated by mirth from the voice of doom
Have I through the pseudo of my mind created my own fate?
How much farther do I need to go before I reach the point of no return?
The far away voice is telling me to choose now before it is too late
I am now seeing the beginning of my demise
and it is not surrounded in glory
Do I stay in this free fall and land somewhere I could never "*BE*"?
YESSS? NOOO!!! I scream.
A voice from within is telling me I have not yet *lived* the life I have chosen
Tears filled with fear are tearing at my eyes
Somewhere within my apathetic self, I am seeing a vestige of light
I focus then walk with trepidation into my future with
the experiences of my yesterdays as my guide
I know my yesterdays experiences give me the
leverage I need to hold me in the now
I am ready to acknowledge I was holding my light at bay
I was blinded by my self-destructive self-pity to see
I am the only cog in the wheel of my life
I am and always will be the only conduit for my light
I acknowledge that I, and only I, am responsible
for the plight of my light and me!

THE DEMISE OF ME - A KANGAROO!

My roots go back to a time where people cared
about each other and my ancestors.
People understood therefore cared about the earth and its inhabitants.
People understood the meaning of abundance was
not related to money or possessions.
These people enjoyed the earth and nature, just because.
We the marsupials, animals, reptiles, insects and rodents love the
earth with a passion that seems to have passed many humans by.
There were people who understood and loved us and
they carry the label as we do of indigenous.
The indigenous species are the salt of the land.
We carry the secrets and idiosyncrasies of earth within our DNA.
My only understanding of anything indigenous is *Australian*.
I know this land has been known by other names *but* my lineage
in my understanding only goes back as far as anthropoids?
This is open to be questioned but I only know what I know.
I know deep within myself that my truth is not necessarily your truth.
I know over time my species has created a hierarchy so
the strong of will, will control the strong of body.
I am so sad because previously we never needed a hierarchy as we lived
by a code of love and understanding of every race, creed and creature.
We respected, nurtured and grazed on the land and in doing so
we were aware of the difference between baron and fertile.
We knew what belonged to who, so respected each and every
individual for their contribution to the worth of and for all.
We were aware of and respected our boundaries.
Within each and every one of us we respected and expected the
same, which in hindsight was the beginning of our demise.
Not necessarily the demise of my lineage but the
demise of morals and respect for you and me!
You decided fun could be had in using guns by stealth and
aiming them at creatures who only knew perfection.
These (my family included) knew perfection was by living and respecting
every blade of grass and every mound of dirt we ever trod on.

Bernadette Reynolds

Our school taught us perfection could only reflect perfection.
We were told we were perfect and because of this we
knew we would never destroy our heritage.
Our heritage told of a love so pure for ourselves and our neighbors.
I know what it is like to be free to traverse the
whole of my country *Australia*.
I know what it is like to be confronted by fences
that frizzle their foe to a pulp?
I feel anger from people who do not know me but
will acknowledge me on your coat of arms.
I know what it's like to be shot at from a distance and close up.
I know what it feels like to have my lady with
our baby in its pouch massacred.
My lady was hit by a something that did not respect her beauty.
It travelled at fast pace and after hitting her she
was left paralysed and close to death.
Unbeknown to anyone but her and me she had our baby,
our flesh and blood being nurtured in her pouch.
When I communicated with her she was circumspect about her peril.
She knew times were still changing and there was nothing
her and I could do to change this sad fact.
We were mother and father of a child who would never see the light
of day but knew the light within of a loving mother and father.
In this moment I knew the depth of doom and gloom,
so for me there was only one way of escaping this world
to rejoin the only family I would ever have.
I know my time is up now so lo and behold here comes a looker of a
car ("GOLD" is the color and GOLD is my reward) so here I go.
WHAM BAM thank you sir because you have allowed
me to be with my bride and my child forever!

BLACK AND WHITE OR COLORS

HOW DO YOU SEE YOUR LIFE?

DO YOU SEE THINGS AS BLACK AND WHITE OR AS COLORS?

If you see everything as black and white are you prepared to bring a little color into your life? Do you judge others through your black and white right or wrong? Do you set yourself up as a critic in the belief of you having every answer for yourself and others?

WHO PERMITS WHO TO DO WHAT, WHERE AND WHEN?

Who has permission to tell another person whether they are right or wrong? Do you firmly place yourself in a position where there's no room for flexibility? Do you fear your beliefs shifting even slightly to inadvertently throw your equilibrium into chaos? Do you then find yourself back pedaling at speed? *WHY?*

I felt I had to justify everything I said and did when I lacked confidence in me. I felt I had to explain the ins and outs of everything I did. This was evident when I purchased a new article as I would characteristically feel the need to explain where I purchased it and what it cost. I was color trying to squeeze myself into black and white.

I would not allow myself to enjoy my life. Many occasions I found myself rummaging and floundering around on the back seat of my car. It took courage for me to open the rear door, get out, then open the driver's door and get in to place myself firmly behind the steering wheel. I then gave myself permission to open my eyes then drive the car in a direction of my choosing.

I then allowed myself to drive in whatever direction I chose to take me out of my black and white and into a rainbow of colors. When I landed on earth I was full of colors then reality knocked on my door so I deferred to the black and white. I sulked and skulked due to my expectations on arrival being thrown into disarray.

A VERY BUMPY RIDE

This is when the full awareness of my decision to come to earth and further my learning made itself clear to me. I was here to overcome every obstacle I had not been able to in previous lifetimes. I chose this journey because it was what I needed to enhance my spiritual. I may have anticipated a cushy journey but it didn't start too promising. There was no soft landing from where I was falling from.

My life alternated between fog then black and white as I was to learn to my detriment. I acknowledge I am a color person who has spent a portion of my life with black and white people. I was berated for being too soft and insecure. With this understanding I would hide everything and deny at any cost. I feared the black and whites so inevitably I attracted them.

Those who live their life through colors are sensitive people. They can be seen by the black and white as insipid and spineless. The black and white minded people cannot comprehend or understand those who see life through colors. I know I articulate a belief of mine to Howard and how I feel about it and he just shakes his head, shrugs his shoulders and continues with whatever it is he is doing. (Never the twine shall meet?)

WHAT IS THE CRITERIA FOR ME TO BE SEEN AS AN ACHIEVER?

I was torn by my expectation for me to be an achiever. As I came to learn I was not academically minded so in class I tended to fly away and play with the fairies. Although when it was time to write an essay or read a book I was totally present. So when I left school why did I take on a job steeped in numbers. I saw myself as insignificant so I shut down my sensitive and creative self.

DOES ANYONE UNDERSTAND ME?

Many creative people have turned to substance abuse when they or their work has not been accepted or understood. Many lived their lives impoverished because their work came from their core (feelings) and not the head (mind). I certainly would not put myself in that category but I understand how a lack of acknowledgment as a person can bring on feelings of insecurity and vulnerability. Without confidence and self-esteem I was left with a gaping hole where my assets should have resided.

HOW PRECIOUS ARE OUR CHILDREN?

Children have great expectations foisted upon them by a society that knows the importance of additions and subtractions. Then as we grow older and somewhat wiser even greater expectations are put on the expertise of the mind. Children can be dragged into a rigid system where the academic regime is seen as more important than the artistic.

I have seen many changes in my life and none more so than the children of today. I have two grandsons, one is eight and the other three. It never ceases to amaze me what these children can do. Both very sensitive and thinking boys who show compassion for people and animals. The art of conversation is alive and well around these two loving and caring individuals. Life seen through their eyes has color and clarity that takes me to the place where my inner child resides.

SCHOOL

The school system has been geared up to accept students coming from the head rather than the heart. *But* now that is changing in as much as children are not graded as they used to be. The sporting field is for learning and having fun and not win at any cost. My eldest grandson participates in little athletics and the care these children show each other puts adult's antics to shame. He is involved in other sports as well where the emphasis is on playing and not win at all costs.

The rigidity of a conventional school cannot be compared to the school of life! The school of life allows us to be our own teacher while simultaneously being a student. For every teacher there are students who want to learn everything they can about life. The school of life does not give answers it challenges the individual to research and come to their own conclusions.

CONVENTIONAL -V- NATURAL?

I heard a doctor/professor speaking the other day about the breakthroughs natural medicine is making into a market held to ransom by conventional medicines. Natural medicine is helping people where conventional medicine has not been able to. We must acknowledge that natural remedies are not combatants in a war between the two. There is room for both and only you can choose for you which path you want to walk. Ultimately when people take responsibility for themselves and their health there will be little need for any artificial medication.

HAVE YOU LOST THE PLOT?

Many people are seen to be losing the plot. This may be because we are trying to live our life from someone else's rule book. We can then find ourselves second guessing everything we do. So why do we get sucked into then give credibility and our energy to a person other than ourselves. This has connotations of our losing direction in our life because if I am not walking your path I must be lost. We can never lose the direction we must take for ourselves in our life because *the grass is not or ever will be greener on the other side.* When we choose to walk our own path there will always be a light at the ready to guide us in the direction we need to go.

HOW HEAVY DOES MY BURDEN BECOME BEFORE I REALISE I AM CARRYING YOURS AS WELL AS MINE!

People who live in the reality of black and white invariably know where their lives are heading and where they will be in ten years time. They will fight tooth and nail for their beliefs as their fear of being out of step with their peers could set them up for ridicule. They can inadvertently look for acceptance from others rather than themselves. These people can find themselves dealing with varying control issues especially when it comes to being a passenger in someone else's life.

People who see life through a kaleidoscope of colors have an awareness of the black and whites but that's about all. They stake their claim to peace in deference to fights and arguments. Feelings are the barometer for a color person so this makes them fearful of moving outside of what feels right for them. They can also surreptitiously find they hold onto outmoded ideas and ideals without realising they are doing so. There is no right or wrong where colors are concerned because they all contribute to the learning we are all here for.

WHO JUDGES AND CRITICISES? NOT ME!

There are many steps to take before we find then understand what is real for us. We have a place within that can be perceived as small and counterproductive or large and out of control. When this place within is out of balance we give ourselves permission to look at, then judge and criticise those who do not see life as we do.

We may believe we have all the answers but unbeknown to us hidden behind a veneer of what we perceive as truth, sits a narrow and limited perspective of life. We can build as many walls with doors around ourselves as we want but in reality this leads us to being sanctimonious in sanctifying ourselves by judging and criticising others.

DO I HAVE A COMFORT ZONE?

I must have a comfort zone because I know at times I want to keep myself exactly where I am. I believe if I move out of my comfort zone my walls then the foundations will crumble. This can only come about when everything I have built my beliefs on turns from rock to sand.

WHAT IS YOUR FOUNDATION BUILT ON?

We have to acknowledge our only salvation is to put down new foundations for us to build our life on. For myself I found the black and white did not work because I could never fit into a mould where my mind had supremacy over my heart. I kept fighting against myself when colors would present themselves to me.

I believed for me to survive in this world I had to be black and white. No wonder my foundations kept crumbling when I trusted anyone but me. I would find myself grasping at something then when I thought I had it firmly in my hands it would dissolve into nothing.

INSECURITY IN GROUPS? OR GROUPS OF INSECURITIES?

When individuals come together as a group there is a plethora of insecurities and fears. How easy is it to hide our individual fears and insecurities behind the solidarity of a group? We socialise, work and have fun with these people because I am who they presume me to be. There will always be a pecking order in this group but who cares? Individuals crave attention and will strive for power and recognition which is a trade mark of a *black and white* mind set.

What happens when this group for one reason or another disbands? Where does this leave you? You are aware you need to be cautious when meeting new people because you want them to like you. Did you find when you were a member of your previous group you sat back then judged others from your perspective? You never wanted to stand up and be counted so you kept yourself busy hiding behind the person in front of you.

There are many insecure people who want to be seen but not on their own. They prefer to be seen as a part of a group even if it goes against their beliefs because they do not believe in who they are. Like minded people gravitate to each other and this gives them the confidence they need to criticize others. You will never be the lone voice in a crowd because you will be too busy *fitting in*.

WHO IS YOUR ROLE MODEL AND WHAT MIND SPACE DO THEY LIVE IN?

Were your role models in the black and white mind space? People can be manipulated when they are not flexible especially when they take on a cause they are told is the right one for them. This certainly happens in religions, cults and many more. Due to a person not knowing who they are they can be manipulated in to believing exactly what they are told. These people then truly believe in something that is a far cry from their inner truth.

How many people are discouraged from believing in themselves? This is because the leaders of a group need the power they have over others to feed their ego. Not all groups have this mind set but far too many do. It is up to the individual to start to think for themselves and live by their own truth and not someone else's lies.

NURTURE YOURSELF BECAUSE NO ONE ELSE CAN

How well are you nurturing yourself? Are you open to receiving gifts from people who care about you? Do you try to control others to satisfy your own misguided needs? Are you prepared to forgive yourself for any wrong turns you have taken in your life?

Do you point your finger at everyone you perceive to have done the wrong thing by you? If so when are you going to live your life to your inner rules? You will never nurture yourself if you do not know who you are. The real you not the facade you show to the world to prove you fit in.

HARK, DO I HEAR A POOR ME APPROACHING?

If we have had a strict and unloving childhood do we then reach an age where we rebel? Who cares about me? Do I care about me? Maybe but I am more interested in blaming as opposed to taking charge of my life. No one understands me so someone must pay.

There can be many reasons/excuses for me being a poor me but in reality this is more about self gratification. A poor me lacks the courage it takes to stand up and say, "I am as important as every other person on this earth". We may come together as one but we are all a unique individual filled with many gifts to share with each other.

WHAT IS POWER?

Power is an intangible belief we can take on to be real. We hear this person or that person is powerful so what? If I do not believe this or that person is powerful then they are not. How can I possibly know what power is when I do not have it within myself?

We have to feel something inside before we understand the meaning of what it is to us. Power comes from within and when you access it you will never hand your power to any person outside of yourself. When I am in my own power and you are in your own we will then power along in our respective lives.

CAN THE NEED FOR FUN LAND ME WITH AN ADDICTION?

At times drugs and alcohol will beckon to us with the presumption they can show us a better life. A life that does not include the precious gifts of *joy happiness fun love* and the freedom to do and have everything we want. Initially substances will show wonders you never thought were possible but this is only a subterfuge for a life of pain, anguish and in many more debilitating afflictions.

BLACK AND LIGHT OR BLACK AND WHITE?

When fossiking around in the dark you realise you need a torch to help guide you with its light. Anger can rear its ugly head when you are groping around in the dark for the torch you know is there but keeps eluding you. What are you really looking for anyway? Find your torch within then you will never have to look for one outside of yourself. Your light within does not need batteries as it works on self-love.

COLOR

Color is flexible, intangible and transcends to inspire and teach us that everything's okay as long as we are in charge of our own life. Color is flow and movement and is not controlled. Color allows us to live our outer life from and with Unconditional Love. Color does not say yes or no but allows us to express and live our life our way.

LIFE IS FOR LIVING!

When we allow color into our lives we open up to the wonders life has to offer. There are so many wonders but unless our eyes are wide open we will never see. Once you see the beauty in yourself you will see it everywhere. Unless you see beauty in every person you meet you will be floundering in a bottomless pit of nothingness.

DID YOU SHOW THEM?

We see things in a different way when our inner-light is switched on. Our vision becomes softer and where there was harshness there is now gentleness.

I never show anyone anything because everything is there for us all to see, we just have to want to.

LET COLORS, COLOR YOUR LIFE?

Let your colors mix with my colors and then with their colors to create of world filled with color. Make sure you leave plenty of room for black and white because we need to keep ourselves grounded. Colors v black and white are our yin and yang so it is up to us all to make sure we all work together in harmony.

For any one of us to be fully in the now we have to integrate our colors with the black and white. Only then can we be a whole person who sees everything from every perspective. There can be no right or wrong because everything just is!

AFFIRMATION

I WILL BRING NEW COLORS INTO
EACH AND EVERY DAY
OF MY LIFE
I WILL CHERISH EACH AND EVERY ONE OF MY COLORS
MY COLORS WILL BRING PROSPERITY
AND ABUNDANCE
INTO MY LIFE!

MOTHER EARTH

My footsteps are heavy so someone must pay
My inner voice says I will rue the day
As sure as the phoenix will rise
I plot my own demise
I curse and swear to my heart's content
My beauty and love is now buried in cement
I am beholden to none
I say therein lies the fun
I say my duty is to appease for my own greed
This is what my morals have decreed
I say I reserve the right
Then like a thief I stealth in the night
I plunder and pillage
Then make sure there is no spillage
I impose on others space
Then make sure my tracks have no trace
My light has now gone out
This I surely have no doubt
I am the expeditor of my doom
For a conscience there is no room
Will death and despair be my final hurrah?
NO!!!!!!!!!!!!!!!!!!
Because Mother Earth has already been this far
She *is* the eternal survivor!
She *is* her own driver!

TRANQUILITY IN THE NIGHT

There is but a whisper in the night
My heart is listening with pure delight
The creatures of the night are singing in tune
To the wise old father moon
Trees stand tall
Guarding their all
Their secrets are many for all to share
I am assured there is no room for despair
There is no need for the eyes to be congealed
When the heart is open all is revealed
The night is so still
I breathe in my fill
The whisperings of the night are truly alive
Telling me that I will survive
The whisperings of nature are here to be shared
The messages they impart are to be adhered
Thank you for your great beauty
The secrets you share are not your duty
They come from a love deep within
I take it in with a knowing grin
Your magnificence is second to none
Our hearts will always beat as one
Thank you for the blessings you bestow
My footsteps are light because now I know
Promises come from heaven above
My heart flows with unending love!

WHEN THE TEARS COME

WHEN I BEGAN TO OPEN UP AND FACE MYSELF THE TEARS CAME!

Tears are the outlet we have to release and cleanse our emotions to allow us to relieve pain from our mind and body. We can only hold so much inside our body before it says I have had enough! This is when we have to sit quietly take stock of ourselves to learn then know what will bring happiness and contentment into our lives. We have to recognise if we don't take whatever time is required we will manifest disease and illness in our body.

FEARS MANIFEST WHAT?

We manifest our now from our deep-seated fear/s so we have to be totally honest with ourselves and know we create our own reality. There will always be pain around fears so we can either choose to deal with them or not. If not our emotional, physical and mental will be debilitated.

TEARS RELEASE WHAT?

It's important to give our tears the freedom to express then release our emotions. This can be related to waterless waterfalls and streams. Debris builds up when cleansing is halted. Tears express *happiness sadness bitterness pain anger bliss joy laughter anxiety anguish* and so on as their job is to evacuate not evaluate. This does not mean we will be crying needlessly it does mean crying will be necessary.

RELEASE YOUR BLOCKS!

Your mind needs to recognise that it's okay to allow tears to release your blocks. You cannot be the person you aspire to be when you have blocks clogging up your system. Due to our body being predominantly water it's important we allow water to do its job by cleansing and refreshing.

EMOTIONLESS?

This reminds me of a man I know who from birth was conditioned against expressing emotions. He is now approaching sixty five years of age and after his birth he was diagnosed as having a hernia. At that time a baby had to wait until they were older before they could be operated on. Consequently his mother was told to keep him as quiet as possible so no further damage could be done. This baby was not allowed to show emotions due to further damage he could cause himself. Somehow he instinctively knew this so he complied and held his emotions within.

OPERATING ON WHAT?

The operation he required was not performed until he was six years old. We can only imagine how deep his then patterns were set. In his growing years after the operation he stayed within himself and did not rely on anyone for anything. He would not express emotions no matter what situation he was confronted with.

I have found him to be an extremely caring and sensitive man who has a deep sense of compassion for everyone and everything. I know there are people who do not see him in this light but that is as much about them as it is about him. He has an innate sense of honesty and fairness so initially he gives others the benefit of any doubts he may have. He believes in the old saying, *if you give someone enough rope they will hang themselves.*

ARE EMOTIONS TANGIBLE?

Our mind is prepared to do whatever it can to further its domination of our emotional self. Our emotional will sway in one direction then change course to move in another without a reason. Whenever we try to describe our emotions there can be angst. Emotions are intangible and words scarce when relating to feelings.

WHAT IS YOUR ENERGY FIELD?

You express through your energy field as it holds the story of your life's *pain sorrow fun* and *joy*. People who are aware observe then understand the kaleidoscope of pictures beaming from their thoughts. This energy field is your aura. Everything manifests in your aura before it shows up in your physical body. No one needs to be *out there* to see and understand the workings of an energy field.

Many people believe they are their physical body but they could not be more wrong. It's important we are aware of this energy field because it is not self contained. It touches people who are in close proximity to you so whatever you are holding within you encompasses any person within this area. This also means we need to be aware as we can take on someone else's issues as our own.

TEARS, TEARS AND MORE TEARS!

Tears if allowed will wash away all the negatives our body will try to hold onto, if not we will be unable to live our life to its optimum. There is no possible way we can move anywhere when we hold onto and not release the *old*. The *old* will hold on for dear life because that's what it knows.

WHO TURNED THE PRESSURE COOKER ON?

Our body works like a pressure cooker needing to release its steam otherwise it will explode or implode. The pressure cooker being a physical object relies on us to release its steam so the food inside will not explode and paint the *walls ceiling* and *floors* with its contents. Whereas humans have free will so we choose to either implode or explode. The pressure cooker of life should be enough in itself without us creating more unrest in our valuable lives.

SUPPRESSION, SUPPRESSES WHAT?

Many illnesses result from implosion as every aspect of ourselves is affected when we choose not to deal with our fears and insecurities. We manifest diseases of the *body* and *mind* or both when we suppress our emotions. Our mind can play tricks when in a state of confusion then loses the ability to deal with situations or people in a rational manner.

The mind can create debilitating illusions and delusions then become very cunning and play games especially when it is trying to slot itself into a reality where it is in control. The mind does not understand or really care about the emotions in its quest for self-preservation.

DO I NEED TO EXPLODE BEFORE SOMEONE LISTENS TO ME?

Explosion has the opposite effect of implosion and is more debilitating as it brings other people into the equation. When you do not deal with your fears and insecurities you will surely deem other people responsible.

Explosion becomes a reality when you render yourself helpless. You may bring many and varying characters into your life to cover your deficiencies but it never will work. Explosion leaves you with recriminations and many unanswered questions. Why has this, why have I, why are they doing this to me? The ultimate question is why am I doing this to myself?

HIDE, EXPOSE OR IMPOSE?

Our wardrobe can harbour many colourful outfits and associated accessories to camouflage our emotions. The outfits can be well-worn and distorted so will never fit no matter how hard we try to rework them. They have never or will ever fit because we are an individual where one size does not fit all. We have to go within to expose what is hiding so as not to impose on another person.

VICTIM, ADORED OR ABHORRED?

People who have been abused carry the pain their abuse has caused until they deal with every aspect of it. How can they possibly remove themselves from their victim status? Other people have got over theirs but I'm sure it wasn't as bad as mine. Look at them out there laughing and having fun *but* I know that will never be me.

Whatever your belief is you will be right. If you believe you can get over your abuse issues then you will. You will take whatever steps needed to deal with it to move on, in and with your life. If you want to hold onto the pain the abuse has caused you will be stuck in a time warp until you let go. *It may be painful to let go but it is more painful to hold on!*

WHEN DO WE SAY ENOUGH IS ENOUGH!

There undoubtedly will come the time when you say enough is enough! I have had enough of this and I know I deserve to live a more fulfilling life. When this occurs you have to know there are compassionate people who care and are able to help each and every one of us. Ask for and be prepared to receive help because it will be forthcoming. It's only difficult when we hold tightly onto the old broken down model.

DOES AN ABUSER FEEL GUILT?

Some abusers feel guilt and others do not. How many abusers promise they will never do it again? Then how long does it take for them to repeat the same old. Their words may change whereas their behaviour does not. Unless there is remorse walking hand in hand with want the will to change will be a flurry of words without conviction.

KNOW YOUR POWER!

Some victims blame themselves for their mistreatment from an abuser. These victims due to their insecurities can wallow in murky waters while pretending they are clear as crystal. Due to our individual uniqueness there are many and various behavioural patterns we take on for our survival.

There is substance as well as other various means of abuse a victim will use when they find themselves not fitting in. We need to go deep within to access our power to bring about change in our lives. We are powerful but many do not believe in ourselves enough to take charge of our life. This belief must change for each of us to live a rewarding and fulfilling life.

DO I LIVE THE "POOR ME"?

Many artificial tears come with the *poor me* by rendering ourselves weak and helpless and not dealing with our issues and shortcomings. There is plenty of help out there but we have to ask pertinent questions to be directed to the appropriate person/people. Get rid of your delusion and illusion and your attention seeking as this is the trademark of a *poor me*. There can be no room in your life for a *poor me* otherwise you will never reach your full potential to be a well adjusted and contented you.

LIFE IS SIMPLE!

Keep it simple! Everything is simple its only people who complicate things. How many people say *"this is who I am if you don't like it too bad because I am not going to change for anyone."* What a joke because the only person we can change for is ourselves.

Some people surround themselves with victims so they appear to be in control. No one needs to be in control of anyone or anything. We need to let go and just be as there is no balance in your life when you have control issues. Life is simple so simplify rather than complicate then you will live your life as you are meant to.

DO TEARS REPRESENT STRENGTH!

How many people perceive tears render them weak?

My life has been plagued by tears at the ready to reveal themselves with or without my permission. I'm a sensitive and emotional person so tears are a natural for me. When I was seventeen my mother told me I should not let others see me cry because this showed weakness.

I understood her meaning but my body had other ideas and they did not correlate. Tears are released to express when words are inadequate.

SILENT TEARS?

When I suppressed tears I internalised and hid behind a cloak of confusion. I found myself putting on a front to show everyone I was strong. This led me down the path of confusion with a need for acceptance. I played some nasty and hurtful games at this time in my life due to closing off my sensitive self. Well I may have believed I had closed my sensitive self off but this could never be a reality because I was me and not someone else. Every human has feelings so it's imperative for us to learn how to deal with them in a positive as opposed to a negative way for positive results.

THE TRIALS AND TRIBULATIONS OF MY LIFE

I knew I wanted to be seen to fit in so decided to change my body image. I knew if I had the perfect body I could achieve anything. My campaign for perfection and acceptance took on a life of its own. My mind mapped out my strategies for this quest so I began my trek to another dead end. My affirmation at the time was deny and if anyone questioned me a denial was always at the ready.

I did deny. I started off by denying myself food because this surely was the quickest way to lose weight. I soon became bored as I had always enjoyed food so I made friends with bulimia. It did keep the weight off as well as appeasing my appetite and this became my life for many years.

WHERE AND WHEN WOULD I EVER FIND ME?

I was not satisfied (as I should have been) so there had to be more. There certainly was and it came in the form of exercise. I became a gym junkie then progressed to an aerobics junkie. I must say this did keep me busy for a while but there was the ever present space within that could never be filled.

My mind was working overtime to bring new ways to keep me busy so I took to running. I began running short distances and realised I loved the release running gave. I felt I was in control of myself so I began to run longer distances. I did enjoy the freedom this gave me because all I had to do was run and not think.

SADLY MY SESSION BECAME ANOTHER OBSESSION!

As with most things in my life running became an obsession. I found I had to push myself harder, then harder to feel I was gaining anything. At this time I made a decision to run a marathon so I pushed my body and mind until breaking point then some more. I would run many kilometres in the heat of the day and not take in the water my body craved because I had to be strong.

Somewhere amongst all of this I found alcohol to help build my confidence. This it did initially with the promise of greater things to come but it never delivered. It debilitated then handed me a copious amount of pain with guilt thrown in for good measure.

DESTRUCTION IF NOT NIPPED IN THE BUD CAUSES EVEN MORE DESTRUCTION!

The running and the alcohol continued for many years causing destruction and pain to the people closest to me. I was consumed with myself in a very negative way. I had no confidence in myself to take the steps needed to find out the extent of my capability.

My immediate family and close friends stuck by me through thick and thin. They saw beauty in me and would tell me so. How could I believe them when all I saw was a helpless pathetic person who was wasting space being here? They obviously saw something worthwhile in me because their support did not and still has not waivered.

I WAS GOING CRAZY SO I GAVE MYSELF PERMISSION TO CRY

Somewhere inside of me it felt good being like this because I could cry. I could cry when I was drunk, then I could cry the next day when the guilt set in. I welcomed the tears as they relieved me of my pain. It was time to leave my cycle of craziness behind me. My relationship with the people who loved me had been wearing thin but their support was still as strong as ever. I now believe I used this against them so they could feel some of the pain I was in.

I AM RESPONSIBLE FOR ME!

Somewhere along this road I realised I had to change. I was responsible and accountable for me. It was up to me to make the changes I required to function as a whole person, tears and all.

I knew it would be a long and hard road to find something in myself worth hanging onto. I began by taking small but very worthwhile steps. There have been times when I have slipped and fallen but I never went backwards. Rivers of tears keep falling but now they are tears of salvation rather than destruction.

I AM MY OWN JAILER!

I am the person who built my own jail where I existed rather than lived for years. I now realise how blessed I am to have had the wherewithal to release myself. The me who can cry whenever and wherever I am because crying is a basic release for us all.

I know everything has to come from within as this is the only way we can make any sense of ourselves. People can give me words of encouragement *but* it is up to me to do the time.

My heartfelt thank you goes to the wonderful people who have believed in and loved me even when I had no idea of what love was. I have since realised I never needed to run a marathon because *I AM RUNNING THE MARATHON OF LIFE ITSELF.*

AFFIRMATION

I AM ME
HOW LUCKY AM I
I AM IT ALL
I AM CONNECTED TO IT ALL
I AM IT ALL
I AM ME!

UNDERSTANDING

KEEP YOUR LIGHT SHINING
BECAUSE YOU NEVER KNOW
WHERE DARKNESS IS LURKING!

RECIPE

STUBBORNESS IS SELF-SERVING
SO WHEN THE OLD INGREDIENTS
NO LONGER WORK FOR YOU
THROW THEM OUT AND
EXPERIMENT WITH NEW ONES!

THE POWER OF UNCONDITIONAL LOVE

There is no greater power than the power of *unconditional love*. *Unconditional love* penetrates every person and place to bring light where darkness hides. The wonder of *unconditional love* means you can project it outside of yourself to anyone and everyone. There are no boundaries where *unconditional love* is concerned only the boundaries and restrictions we create for ourselves.

Before we are a seed planted in our mother's womb we are *unconditional love*. Our being is *unconditional love* so when do we forget? When do we begin to get caught up in scarcity, misery and pain to forget we are *unconditional love*? Have you ever experienced the inner glow of *unconditional love*? This inner glow brings with it many wonders with attachments of enchantment *joy bliss courage trust peace harmony* and a realisation of us all being one.

MY JOURNEY TO SELF-REALISATION

I would challenge people to tell me who I was, where I was going and how I was getting there. I never bothered to look in the one place where my *unconditional love* was glowing continually. I blamed then accused and cursed every obstacle on my path to make you, then you responsible for my journey. I tread the old boards of every person who was there before me. I never bothered to look down to see how worn out these boards were. I kept looking around me to find someone to latch onto to take my pain away and then blame them for my plight.

I deemed myself powerless in a world requiring me to be confident and self-assured. Instead of accessing my light of *unconditional love* I used alcohol, cigarettes and every other excess I could find for my survival. I was floundering and flaying around like a fish caught on a fishing line. There was no rhyme or reason to anything I was doing. I was staggering around in the dark trying to find what, I will never know, because I never found it. I found myself exploring places on my hands and knees with my eyes closed then would end up covered in cobwebs.

This was my life for many years and three times I tried to relieve myself of any further exploring. I finally took myself by the hand and began my journey within. Initially my heart was closed so the road ahead promised to be long and lonely and it delivered because it lived up to my expectations.

When I let go of the baggage I had accumulated over many years I began to experience *unconditional love* of and for myself. I gave my ego a rest and asked my heart to guide me to know and understand my purpose. I came to realise there were many other people trudging their way through their life as I was. It was time for me to be authentic by offering my hand of friendship to help someone who wanted to access their inner light of *unconditional love.*

I needed to ask me why I kept myself in hiding and ignorant for so many years. I had to take responsibility for everything I put myself and people who loved me through. I really believed I was fooling people but I could not have been more wrong because they were not fooled at all. These people were showing me *unconditional love* and I never saw it. I believed they would be better off without me but they were at the ready with a safety net to catch me every time I fell.

I had no idea of this until I woke up. I looked at these people and saw the scratches and scars, the dust in their hair from where they were following me. They had lost a lot of the original sparkle in their eyes but nothing deterred them from giving their all to be there for me. It took me a long time before I could acknowledge what these wonderful people had done.

I drank myself to every possible place I could go. Initially the places were promising but soon turned to a mega disaster. I had reasons and excuses at the ready but every time I accessed one I would take myself further away from the person I was here to be.

I had to eat humble pie when the realisation of myself finally dawned on me. I learned many valuable lessons from my experiences but in the long term the proof was going to be in the eating of the pudding. Can I sustain my now belief in every aspect of myself for the duration of my life?

I am in wonder and overjoyed with the inspiring feelings I now have due to these people. My unconditional love for my family brings with it many blessing as will never take anything for granted. I find myself tearing up just thinking about these beautiful people. I love being in their company and knowing I am exactly where I am meant to be. They have accepted me with open arms without so much as a recrimination or a sideways glance.

I also realise I am here because of me. Somewhere within I decided it was time to change my direction in life. As many people who have treaded these boards will know there are gaps to fall through as well as solid boards to walk on. I know I had to stay focused in the now because as soon as I looked back I stumbled and sometimes fell but somehow managed to pick myself up and continue on.

I came to realise there are no certainties outside of myself. My only certainty is that my body was born into a physical world and will be despatched in a physical world whereas my spirit is eternal.

How many people are floundering their way through life hoping? As the old saying goes *hope springs eternal*. What does hope mean for you? You need to do more than hope. You have to move beyond hope for you to grow both spiritually and emotionally. You could spend your whole life hoping until eventually you forget what it is you are hoping for. Your life is precious so make it count for something more than hope. You are unique so share your uniqueness in a positive way to create a better world for us all.

Do not pretend you are doing this and that for someone else because in reality you cannot unless you do it for yourself first. Do not hide behind awards and accolades and cheers of *they are a jolly good fellow* unless you can sing it about yourself first. Unless you access your inner light of *unconditional love* you have nothing real. You can tell yourself whatever story you want to hear but it changes nothing. So please give yourself the greatest gift of all, the gift of you to yourself by understanding the *POWER OF YOUR UNCONDITIONAL LOVE*.

RECIPE

LOVES POWER TAKES ME TO MY HIGHEST PEAK
THEN WITHOUT RHYME OR REASON
I CAN FIND MYSELF AT MY LOWEST EBB
THE CRUX COMES WHEN I AM NOT CENTERED
THEN FIND MYSELF FLOATING
SOMEWHERE IN BETWEEN
SHOULD I LOOK UP, DOWN OR AROUND
THERE IS ONLY ONE PLACE TO LOOK
AND THAT IS WITHIN BECAUSE
THE POWER OF UNCONDITIONAL LOVE IS WITHIN
THEN AND ONLY THEN CAN I SHARE THE
POWER OF MY *UNCONDITIONAL LOVE*
WITH EVERYONE AND EVERYTHING
BECAUSE ULTIMATELY

I AM *UNCONDITIONAL LOVE!*

SHAPE SHIFTER YASMAN

Yasman is a ten week old Jack Russell pup who
has recently entered into our lives.
In the two weeks we have had her she has shifted
and rearranged every shape in our lives.
Jasper our five and a half year old Jack Russell
has had his privacy stolen from him.
Astral our nearly five year old cat has been relegated to hiding behind
doors and sitting on chairs previously not in his consciousness.
Dinnertime is not the peaceful experience for the animals as it used to be.
Astral has to be locked in the laundry for some peace and quiet while eating
his meal and Jasper has to fight for every mouthful of food he consumes.
Underclothes are not safe and are developing holes within the
blink of an eye and under our constant surveillance.
Puncture holes seem to be manifesting in our
body without any obvious cause.
Our only reality is of a tornado barking and growling
and leaving in its wake mass destruction.
Ornaments and fixtures have been *moved, dislodged,*
chewed, pulled apart and in some cases lost.
I realise I was not tuned into them because they obviously were
not happy where they were. So I have to thank Yasman for
coming into my life and showing me the error of my ways.
Sleep deprivation goes with the territory especially now I am getting up
two to three times a night to take her outside for her constitutional.
In the morning my eyes will not open through lack of sleep
so I fossick around for my dressing gown only to find myself
stumbling onto one of her gifts she thoughtfully left for me.
Do not think for one moment I am not appreciative of her gifts.
I'm sure I am but in my reasoning gifts should be presented to me
rather than hidden and left for me to step on with bare feet.
Then when I have showered and cleaned all evidence of her gift
from my person it is time to play treasure hunt. I have to search the
house high and low for every other present she has left for me.
She yells, screams and throws tantrums when things do not go her way.

Jasper never dug holes but she does.
When she goes outside with Jasper she gets him upset
which in turn sets the neighborhood dogs going.
They sing in unison a song so mournful where ear muffs are
our only respite from their ear shattering performance.
Jasper the male has relinquished his peace and quiet
for Yasman the female. (sound familiar guys.)
Yasman is without a doubt the dominant fixture
in his life at this present time.
Astral treats her with the contempt only a cat can.
Oscar the budgie sits on his perch and sees all but gives nothing away.
Howard is suffering from sleep deprivation because Yasman
has chosen him to be her pillow, scratching board and teeth
sharpener so now he is existing as opposed to living.
I, on the other hand do not know where I am because my life is
changing from minute to minute, then demand upon demand.
Yasman is taking me to a puppy preschool tomorrow night.
I know she will show me up to be an inadequate Yasman owner
but after everything I have been through I will soldier on.
I know every insecurity I have will be brought out for everyone to see.
I will be put through the hoops while she combs her hair, applies her
mascara and lipstick to leave me sitting like a lone figure on a rock.
I will be deemed an incompetent owner who has no
idea of teaching a puppy the important things for their
growth to be a well-rounded and secure dog.
I know my pleas of competency will fall on deaf ears because
the teacher by looking at me will know I have been around
the block many times and I should know the score.
Yasman has already learnt to batt her eyelids at every
male and female for attention so how can I possibly
compete with something so small and innocent.
I find myself stumbling and stammering when trying to cover
my inadequacies. I have to ask myself *why does something that*
fits into my once slipper have the ability to shift and reshape the
lives of people who have been around for many years?
As I am writing this she is lying beside Jasper in front of
the heater and is comfortable but I know in her sleep she
is planning her next strategy to bring me down.

My inner voice is telling me she is preparing for another onslaught tonight.
I have spoken too soon because once again she is
asserting her supremacy over Jasper and myself.
She is telling him off the same way a fish wife does her husband.
Jasper sadly has surrendered once again to her dominant behavior.
One moment he was chewing a bone then after she
abused him for five minutes the bone was hers.

She has come into our lives for a reason but at the moment I have to question my sanity in thinking a pup would breathe new life into our home.

I dearly hope she is not only here to dominate and dictate to us because if she is I will have to sit down and put in place a new set of strategies. I will not have a pint size ball of energy ruling my life. As for Howard he loves without setting boundaries around suitable or unsuitable behavior. I know this is surely another job a woman must do.

Yasman is certainly a shape shifter and I would not want her to be any different as she is being true to herself and goes with her instincts.

She has brought *fun laughter joy love pain* and *injury* into our lives but we love her dearly.

THE CONTINUING STORY OF YASMAN

Life fell into some type of normality with our two dogs and one cat. Yasman respected Jasper from a distance and Astral from a greater distance. When she got jealous of Jasper she would become very aggressive with him and it unnerved Howard and I greatly. Eventually I decided the best thing to do for us all was to try and re home her.

DOG ANYONE?

I spoke to my daughter of what I wanted to do for all our sanity so she said she would put her on Facebook for me. I was torn because I loved her but I also loved the others so I said yes. I also believed she was being looked after from the other side so I knew only someone who really wanted her would take her. I was certainly right on that score because she wasn't going anywhere at any time. No one put their hand up to take her so we had to dig even deeper to find a solution.

WHO WHISPERS?

This is when I decided in my infinite wisdom to employ a dog whisperer. In the long run she had me well trained whereas for Yasman it was business as usual. I also put her in a dog care centre a couple of days a week. Eventually she was attending only one day a week.

There was a lovely and caring young man who worked there and he took Yasman under his wing. He advised me that Yasman didn't fit in because she did not like other dogs. He said she is a wonderful human dog but definitely did not cut it as a dog's dog, so, back to the drawing board.

FENCED IN, NOT ME

We walked a long and tedious line keeping us in suspense for a long time. I loved Yasman dearly and only wanted the best for her and the others. It was about this time when we decided to move house. We purchased our property in the country but were in a dilemma when it came to Yasman. We knew Jasper and Astral would settle in but Yasman is a very different story (or so we thought). I kept trying to visualise where we could put up a fence to keep Yasman in. Our property it's almost impossible to fence in a city dog who was used to having the run of the back yard as well as the house.

The previous lightbulb had not been extinguished because once again I thought it would be better if we tried to re home Yasman. I just could not see how she would possibly fit into life on a property. Well nothing came of my idea so moving day arrived. The truck was packed to overflowing and with cat in cage and dogs safely tucked away in the car, it was time to go. I had been making a lot of promises to a lot of angels for this to work out so only time would tell.

YASMAN THE GREAT

Eventually we arrived and the time of reckoning came when we let Yasman out of the car. It was a beautiful experience because Yasman looked out over our property and said, *at last I am home*. From that moment she has loved and protected the property as if she owned it.

Initially there were some friendly ducks on the edge of the water and she began to bark at them. Howard went over to her and said *NO. He* explained that these ducks were welcome here and she was not to harm them in any way. (dog people would understand where he was coming from.) Howard also had to explain to her that kangaroos were also a part of the environment we now lived in so she must keep clear of them. The only thing he has told her not to protect and that's the foxes because they will kill the friendly as well as native ducks.

Quite often of a night when Yasman barks constantly Howard will pick up his torch then go outside and be confronted with the eyes of a fox. We have diligently cleared our place of undergrowth so there is nowhere a fox can hide. We dismantled some of their dens so they knew we meant business. Yasman knows we have to look after the ones who cannot look after themselves so she has taken on this mantle and has worn it with great pride.

When kangaroos are around she will walk right past them without giving a second glance and they seem to be mesmerised by her. It is so beautiful to see them watching as she walks past them because she is an unknown to them and they seem to be intrigued by her.

WHO WOULD HAVE BELIEVED?

Since Jasper passed over she has become a beautiful, loving and confident dog. She and Astral have called a truce and life with them both is wonderful. Somehow Yasman knew the day I bought her she would eventually be living here because she has been the perfect dog for where we are. She knows the boundaries of our property and protects them with her all.

GREEN CAN BE DANGEROUS

After taking possession of our house and property I was very green in every way especially when it came to clearing the property. With Yasman by my side and my trusty wheelbarrow and axe I went on my crusade. An axe was not my usual tool of trade so I was a bit of a cowboy as Yasman was to find out.

Pieces of wood were flying here, there and everywhere until Yasman realised she would either need a hard hat or protect me from the comfort of a chair strategically placed on our verandah. She loved her now life therefore wanted to live for many more years to come.

These days when I venture out (a lot the wiser I may say) she escorts me to where I am going and will then unobtrusively crisscross her way to our verandah hoping I will not notice she has gone. There is no way I can convince her I have now mastered the axe and she does not need to be in fear for her life. She has also seen the way I drive our little tractor and is prudent enough to walk far enough away from me to know she is out of harm's way.

MORE LESSONS = MORE LEARNING

Yasman accompanies me on my morning walk which she loves. Initially I let Yasman walk off lead as I believed she was then free. In my finite wisdom I carried her lead, just in case. Well there I was confronted with another off lead dog with another apologetic owner. I would call her to me but she forgot how to hear me even when she could see me.

I would stand there calling then yelling at her to come back to me but she was far too busy. Oh, I still had so much to learn particularly when she happened to be confronted by other dogs. Her disdain for other dogs was obvious when she was snapping and snarling while waiting for me to protect her. I must have looked silly while trying to apologise for Yasman's behavior while I had the control I needed in my hand (lead). In reality it was my behavior in question and not Yasman's because she was true to herself whereas I was not true to anyone including myself.

I thought I was doing what Yasman wanted but in reality it was only my perception of what she wanted as I was to find out. I then decided it was time to put her lead on when we approached the walking track. I once again realised how wrong my thinking was because Yasman loved being on the lead. She walks at a steady pace and does not veer off the track. She doesn't intimidate other dogs so we both have a smile on our respective faces.

This has been another valuable lesson for me because I believed she was free when she was off her lead. Whereas in actual fact it was taking her to somewhere she had not experienced so she did not know how to react. When we lived in Melbourne she was used to going for walks on her lead therefore when she was leadless she was confused as to what was expected of her.

I now believe the more I learn the less I know. I make sure I put on my L (Learning) plates before I leave the house to go anywhere. Yasman has certainly been wonderful for me. Ever so slowly she has guided me out of my tunnel vision into a world where anything is possible as long as I am prepared to be open to learn.

Yasman is now nine and a half years old and is the most wonderful companion I could have ever asked for. Every person who owns a pet will know of the trials and tribulations of owning one. *But* there can be no price put on what they give in return. She loves me unconditionally even though I tried to have her re-homed. In retrospect it was a journey we both needed to further our growth as human and dog. She has taught me many things about life and living. She has taught me to trust in myself instead of second guessing and coming up with a blank.

I thank Yasman for being in my life and allowing me to just, be me.

THE JANET PLANT

What is the Janet plant? You may well ask
This plant's unique flower emits an unidentifiable
perfume to tease our senses
Its foliage is representative of the perfection of earth
It radiates love and light from the depths of its core
The brilliance of its colors has no comparison
Its ambience is synonymous with the purity of life
Its characteristics can only be compared to an
ocean ebbing and weaving with the tides
Its ever changing tides flow like the idiosyncrasies of life
The perfume emitted by this flower can only be recognised by few
The plant and its flower is timeless so will leave you wondering
Wondering if anyone has ever witnessed this
plant reaching its full potential?
The Janet plant will only be acknowledged and loved by those who see
If you do not see then you must ask yourself WHY?
"It's your fault because you are hiding this plant from me!"
"I would surely recognise it if I saw it, wouldn't I?"
Only those who are open to this plant will know
Because its roots lie within each and every one of us
I hold the reality of this plant deep within me
Its fragrance guides me every moment of every day
What about You?

**THE BEAUTY OF THE JANET PLANT WILL LIVE IN
YOUR HEART UNTIL YOU MOVE INTO ITS REALITY.**

A TREE'S LIFE

THE BEGINNING

The first memory I have is being picked up then flown until I was dropped to land somewhere. I tried very hard to see what was around me but I was just too small. I felt something hard land on me and I was pushed down into a dark and cold place. There was nothing I could do so I lay there wondering what I was and what would become of me. Something deep within knew it was a lesson about patience *but* I thought what else could I possibly do when I was lying there helpless.

As I was involved in my lesson in patience time went by and I was none the wiser as to who or what I was or so it would seem. Until the day came when a miracle occurred because I felt myself moving and growing from the bottom of me as well as the top. I could feel myself going deeper and deeper into the dark that was holding me in place. From the top of me I pushed through the dark and began to see and feel lighter.

I had made my way out of the dank of the dark into the freshness of light. I tried very hard to observe what was around me but all I could feel was myself swaying (well it was a slight movement anyway). I had a realisation that what was holding me deep into the darkness was important for me to stay in the light to continue growing.

ONE OF MANY

The part of me that was in the dark was growing deep and strong to hold me in place while the top of me was growing taller. I began to notice a world I was not familiar with as there were bits and pieces of many and varied things around me. Then the time came when I realised I was not on my own. As I was to discover there were trees surrounding me as well as dirt leaves and grass. I began to put things together to come to the understanding of having landed on dirt, and then someone stood on me and pushed me into the dirt where I began to grow.

I learned this from the trees surrounding me who I came to realise must have been intelligent to know so much. These trees would laugh at and make fun of me because I was not one of theirs. How was I supposed to know this because I could see them but I couldn't see me? I thought I was doing really well as I was growing stronger every day and all my needs were met.

These trees informed me that they had a purpose and I didn't seem to *but* this was only their perception of me and not my reality. I will admit my body was not quite like theirs as my trunk branches and leaves had very little in common with theirs. This left me feeling sad and bewildered because I didn't know me so what did I need to do to fit in.

VISITORS

I observed tiny little creatures walking around me while others were flying above as well as around me. They indicated they would come and partake of things they needed from me to help sustain them for their existence. They said I had much to offer the numerous varieties of creatures around but they would wait until I was bigger and stronger. I was feeling sad because I had a need to be needed until I remembered the message relating to patience. So I put on a brave face and sat slept and observed the world around me. Well what else was I supposed to do?

BECOMING AWARE

Time moved on and I kept growing taller and taller until I could see far into the distance. I was mesmerised by the sights, smells and beauty surrounding me. I felt the force of the wind blowing me here, there and everywhere or so it seemed. My trunk was slowly swaying my limbs were dancing to their own tune and my leaves moved to their own tempo. The warmth of the sun's rays infiltrated every part of my being. I felt so at peace with myself and the world that I wanted this feeling to last forever *but* we know don't we that nothing lasts forever?

Some of the community of trees communicated with me while others chose to ignore me. I was informed by the communicative trees that they were fruit trees and their purpose was to stay healthy because they needed to produce fruit for people to eat. I began to get excited because I thought if I tried hard enough maybe I could also produce fruit. I told them what I intended to do and I was laughed at. They said I was scrawny and my limbs were pointing in every direction so there would be no chance of me producing fruit. I then had one of those light bulb moments. Maybe if I focused long and hard enough on me producing fruit on myself it will happen. Isn't it true if you picture within yourself what you see yourself as then you can create the picture outside of yourself? Well I sure will give it a go because what have I got to lose?

WHAT IS MY PURPOSE?

I still felt sad and lonely because I didn't have a purpose. In my leisure time (which was all the time) I watched the fruit trees move in unison to a melody foreign to me and their beauty was breathtaking. I would catch me feeling sorry for myself in the belief I was neglected when the fruit trees were being given abundant attention. They were trimmed and nurtured while the dirt they were standing in was worked until it was in pristine condition. I just loved the smell of the dirt after it had been worked. In fact I loved many smells even though I didn't know where they originated. Oh I really did enjoy the experience of sniffing and being.

The fruit trees told me of the four seasons and what to expect from each one of them. The first season mentioned was the long days when the sun would shine for many days in a row with little rain water to quench our thirst. Then following that season the days would get shorter and cooler and the leaves would fall off the trees leaving them bare and fragile. The next season would be cold and rainy and the days would become shorter so this is the perfect time for me to store as much water as possible to keep me going through the hot months. Then the following season there would be beautiful blossom flowers appearing then they would be followed by new leaves and fruit. I realised I was none the wiser as I didn't produce fruit so where do I fit into this whole scheme of things? I suppose I will have to wait and see and in the meantime I'll just keep picturing myself producing fruit!

Whenever the humans tended to the fruit trees they kept threatening to cut me down and dispose of me. I didn't have a purpose and they couldn't make money out of me. They would laugh and say I was an embarrassment to them and myself and I was not even worthwhile burning. By this time I was extremely sad because I didn't know what sort of tree I was.

MAKING FRIENDS

One day a bird in its wisdom landed on me, then lo and behold another one joined it. They began to chatter and chortle between themselves making me very excited. They told me trees like me were few and far between and how thankful they were having found me. They were not interested in the fruit trees because they are too prissy and did not like them. They informed me they had a very well connected grape vine working so would be able to tell other birds about me. When it was time for them to leave they thanked me and said I should expect many others to follow. They certainly lived up to their word because many and varied birds did come to visit.

Some of these birds told me they had to be very careful around the fruit trees because birds were not welcome as they would try to eat the fruit. Many of our brothers and sisters have disappeared while they were found to be fossicking around the fruit, so as you can imagine we keep our distance. One bird said *I know there is a saying that any life is a good life but we would prefer longevity thank you.* We like you because you are so big and strong and we can sit here and rest while not being seen. I felt totally at peace with any bird sitting on my branches so I thought I would push my luck and ask them what type of tree they thought I was? They just shrugged their little feathered shoulders shook their tiny heads and flew away leaving me none the wiser. Oh well at least I tried!

THE LONG HOT SUMMER

I was feeling really good about myself as I was strong and my roots were holding me firmly in the ground. I loved nothing more than feeling the sun shining down on me while birds were flittering from one branch to another while speaking a language I could not relate to. Then things began to really hot up with no respite. The sun kept beating down on me. The heat was draining and left me feeling very thirsty as the rain seemed to have deserted me. I felt decidedly worse when I saw the fake rain drenching the fruit trees. I asked them about the fake water and once again they laughed at me and said there was no such thing as fake rain. It was water pumped out of a dam to keep them in tip top condition.

They told me I just had to get over it because I had no purpose and was not important like they were. I began to feel my energy being sapped until I no longer cared whether I lived or died. During this time I had to drop a couple of my branches because I could not sustain them with the lack of water. Finally the rain came. I ingested as much of the water as was treely possible to help sustain me and hopefully bring back my zest for life. My roots had become weakened so I had to work very hard at staying strong.

NIGHT MAGIC

One night after a wet day there was a full moon as well as the stars being out. I felt totally cleansed refreshed and loved. I was glowing in the subtle light from the night sky to reflect back exactly what I was receiving. I felt love transpiring between every living thing on the planet in that particular moment. It was as though we were all giving to our father the sky and we were getting back tenfold the joy and bliss it holds within its realms. It was the most amazing feeling I have ever had as I felt I was exactly where I needed to be at that particular time.

LIFE LESSONS FROM AN OWL

I must admit my ego began to do a little dance as I began to see myself as more than I was. During the next day I must have put out some interesting vibes because that night I had a magnificent visitor. I could feel just how intelligent caring and wise this creature was. He introduced himself as an owl.

I was almost blown away (figuratively speaking) in the manner in which this owl conducted his interview with me. I say this because he had many questions where he expected answers. He asked me if there was any one specific question I needed him to answer. At last I had my chance to find out what type of tree I was so I asked him the question. The owl shook its head and asked me why was it so important for me to know because his answer would never give me what I was looking for. If I had to ask then I would never know!

I had no answer to this because I had never thought in this way. I always thought I needed to know where I belonged because I must have had a mother and a father and maybe sisters and brothers. He told me I belonged where ever I was and it was up to me to make the most of my situation because what would I want to change? Did I know or was I trying to appease my curious thoughts?

He asked about my connection to the fruit trees and if I enjoyed their company. I said I felt overwhelmed by them because they had a purpose whereas I didn't. The owl gave me a strange glare and said I was his purpose. Now I was totally baffled because how could someone like me be a purpose for this beautiful creature. He asked me to think about where he was sitting and why? This left me wondering if I had missed some sort of tree school because no answer was forthcoming. Oh well just something else to ponder on.

I then went on to tell him how hard I had tried to be like the fruit trees. When the rain was beginning to come, their leaves would turn beautiful colors and then drop to the ground giving the humans a colorful and cushioned ground to walk on. I told him how I tried very hard to shake my leaves off but nothing ever happened. Then when the sun began to shine they would be adorned by the most beautiful flowers and bees would partake of their nectar. Whereas with me the bees would fly away without giving me a backward glance. Then their leaves would come out in droves to cover their naked limbs and the fruit would begin to grow and ripen for the humans to pick then eat.

He asked me how many birds and little creatures would visit these fruit trees? I had to think very hard and the only answer I could up with was none. The humans would spray the trees with different medicines to keep pests off them. The owl informed me they were not spraying medicines but pesticides so that the fruit would be perfect. Well they may well look perfect but they are not perfect when they need to be sprayed to seem to look and be appertising. You seem to be caught up in how perfect something looks but you have yet to realise just how perfect you are. You have your beautiful trunk limbs leaves and the comfort you give to the many creatures who drop by to say hello.

Your purpose is here to house any one of the tiny creatures who need somewhere to rest when they are tired. You offer comfort and shelter so do not ever underestimate yourself or your purpose. If you were one of those fruit trees I would not be here sitting and talking to you as I am now. You have a presence where they do not. You are an individual who stands out whereas the fruit trees are individuals but as an individual they do not stand out. My purpose with you is now completed so I will bid you goodbye and fly to my next purpose.

But I say as Mr. Owl flies away, you have not told me what type of tree I am. By the time I have finished saying this he is well gone. Now I have a great deal more information to sift through but I'm none the wiser as to my identity or purpose. Word must have spread amongst the birds as to my night visitor and his purpose for spending time with me. I felt the birds respected me more for having been visited by this wisest of creatures. They were throwing questions at me from everywhere but I couldn't come up with a coherent answer.

WHO'S PURPOSE?

In my finite wisdom I asked each and every one of them to tell me their purpose. By this time there were more than birds as other large and tiny creatures were also gathering around me. In unison they said, a *purpose* what's a *purpose*? I replied, *well why are you here, what are you meant to do?* They were scratching their large medium and tiny heads but they could not come up with an answer. They had no concept of anything other than *now*. Everything they did had its own individual purpose because yesterday was forgotten and tomorrow – well who knows? Insects knew they could be swallowed at any moment by a bird but this never deterred them from living every moment to its optimum.

MORE LESSONS FROM A FOUR LEGGED

Seemingly out of nowhere a four legged presented itself to me and said, "I know my purpose and the purpose of every creature here today. It is to live our life with respect for ourselves because when we respect ourselves we will respect all other things on this earth. We respect humans as well as all the variety of plants and trees there are. We respect the water of the world that houses many and varied creatures who have the same rights as you and me.

There are no ifs and buts because there would be no earth without each and every one of us working in unison to make this the beautiful place it is. If I was true to my heritage I would kill or maim you all and think nothing of it, but I choose not to. I choose to eat only when I am hungry and give thanks to the creature who gives his life so I may live. I don't take any of this lightly because

I have learnt no one gains when we take what is not ours. I have chosen the path of respect and it starts with me. If I can't respect me who can I respect?"

With that he was gone and in what direction I would not know but he left behind a precious message for us all. There were an arrangement of oohs and aahs but not much else. Well what could we say? Every one of us who were there learnt a valuable lesson about personal responsibility and accountability. I was living my purpose the whole time but lacked the awareness to know. We were all reminded to continue living our life exactly as we have been but with a greater awareness of all our brothers and sisters. I knew without a doubt we would all be out of balance without each and every one of them.

LIVING WITH PASSION

I realised balance was not just about holding myself erect. It was giving and receiving with love and affection to all. From that moment on I embraced living with a passion that had been dormant in me from my conception. I embraced the sun for its light and warmth so I would not rot away in the depth of darkness. I embraced the clouds filled with their life giving rain so I would not shrivel up and die from continuous light and heat. I embraced the night sky with its ever changing moon and the infinite stars casting their spell over the whole of our planet earth.

This was definitely my epiphany so I then had to ask myself, *what does it matter what type of tree I am because it's how I treat all of you and me that's important.* I realised I have been taking all these other creatures for granted in expecting them to know my purpose. It is up to each and every one of them to know and live their purpose. It is not up to them to know mine as this is my responsibility. I can now look at the fruit trees and respect them for who and what they are. I have my freedom and they have a purpose to produce perfect fruit for humans. We are all in this together but with varying responsibilities to bring balance to our beautiful earth.

MY LIFE COMPLETED

The time is drawing closer for my spirit to leave my purpose on earth as I am feeling tired and depleted of energy. The change of seasons has taken its toll leaving me feeling weak. Due to my learning on earth I know I am strong. I have been privileged to encounter many and varied creatures and every single one of them have left their mark on me. I know my passing will leave a gap in their lives but I also know they respect themselves and this is their purpose. I know I have given protection and shelter when it was needed so what greater purpose could a tree have?

It's time! I can feel myself falling and my limbs breaking off. Without any fuss I feel the force of tree meeting earth complete. I am now spirit and will shortly meet up with my friends who also now live in the spirit world.

MEMORIES

Memories are flooding me with their joy and heartache. I remember when I was introduced to a magpie and he was very cheeky. He would torment me with his quirky sense of humor and love of life. Eventually he brought along his female partner and informed me that I was going to be an uncle. They diligently made a little home on one of my branches to welcome the newest member of their family. As a female magpie only produces one egg each season their attention to every detail was a joy to behold. Once the egg was laid the waiting game began.

The egg had to be kept warm for the baby magpie to grow then emerge from its shell. This was a momentous day for all as this tiny bird emitted a tiny chirp. The parents then had to find food for this tiny bird so it would grow into a strong healthy adult, and this it did. That was the one and only bird to be born on me but every year the extended family would always come to visit and proudly show off their newest offspring. It still brings a tear to me when I think how blessed I was and just how much richer my life was due to this experience.

Then there were a few of the local dogs who chose me to leave their scent on. At the time of them leaving their scent I was not overly impressed but then I came to realise it was like a badge of honor to be thought of in this way. They knew their scent would be around for many more generations of dogs to sniff. Subsequently I did live for many years and made my contribution to humans by breathing out precious oxygen.

There were also the insects who joyfully went about their business. Some were the flying variety and others were land bound but they all knew they could be eaten at any moment, but this never deterred them from living in the now. I learned so much from these tiny beings as they seemed to vibrate on a level all of their own.

Then there were all the other varieties of birds who would come and sit on me and tell me of their joy and sorrow. Some would squabble amongst themselves then would amicably leave to live their purpose. Some would just sit and sing their songs of love and joy to bring a lightness to all who listened. At times a bird would turn up with a chip on its shoulder and try to cause disharmony to all and sundry. At these times a peacemaker bird would appear and give as much help as was needed to assist this bird to live its purpose. Oh the memories aren't they just wonderful.

I certainly cannot forget my friends the fruit trees who I had varying relationships with. Some were envious of me because of my freedom and others were content within themselves so were happy for me. The envious ones were tired of them all being treated the same when they had their own individual personality. They knew they were treated with great respect because they had a job to do. Somehow I know they would have liked to have changed places with me if only for one day to feel the essence of freedom. Initially I thought these trees were stuck up but in actual fact they were lonely even though they were surrounded by many.

REUSE AND RENEW

As I look down to my tiny place on earth I can see a human with a chainsaw cutting my outer body into pieces. Then there is another human splitting and stacking the precious wood to be used to keep a family warm in the winter. It will be used in a beautiful open fire where the family will gather around and share their own stories. They will be warm and safe in the company of each other and this is their purpose. Once I am burnt my ashes will be distributed back to the ground from where I once originated. Maybe, just maybe I might be harboring another minute seed to grow and realise its own purpose!

I never did find out what type of tree I was but do you know I don't care because my life was so enriched in every way possible. I thank all my friends, the owl and the four legged who taught me some valuable lessons.

I NEVER NEEDED TO KNOW, I JUST HAD TO BE!

JASPER AND ASTRAL

Every person who has shared their life with an animal has their own beautiful story to tell and this is mine.

Jasper was a Jack Russell with a short wiry coat to suit his short sturdy legs but with the attitude of a Rottweiler.

Astral is our cat who came to rely on Jasper for his very life.

Jasper was born on 12th January 1999 and Astral was born 26th November 1999.

THE JASPER AND ASTRAL STORY

My track record with dogs was forgettable at best. When I was a child we had dogs but I never really related to them as my siblings did. Howard also did not have much experience with dogs either apart from the fact his father had owned some. From Howard's perspective they were not treated very well. With this in mind he declared he would never own a dog unless he was in a position to look after it properly. Obviously Jasper overlooked our fears and decided he would change our beliefs and this is exactly what he did.

A young friend of ours and his girlfriend had a female Jack Russell and she was having pups. This friend said to me one day that he wanted Howard and I to have one of her pups. These were only a few innocent words but they brought out all mine and Howard's dog fears. Howard and I could not find one good reason why we should have a dog. Our friend was quite adamant about his decision so finally Howard and I succumbed and said we would have one.

The day finally the day arrived when the pregnant mother gave birth to her pups. Our friend suggested Howard and I take a look at them in a few days. I decided it was time for me to check the pups out and due Howard still being at work I went on my own to face our future.

I walked into the house and there was the proud mum and her beautiful little pups. Naturally I fell in love with them but I would never have been able to choose one on my own. When Howard returned home from work I related to him what I had experienced then encouraged him to see them as soon as he possibly could.

A few days later he decided it was time for him to take a look at the pups. Somewhere within him he knew he would not choose one and he was right on that account. When we walked into the house and sat down he was watching the pups who at this time, did not have their eyes open. One particular pup crawled his way around the other pups then made his way over to Howard's foot and that's where he stayed. He had chosen the person he wanted to spend his life with.

With this the mother who was not an overly friendly dog stood in front of Howard then laid on her back for him to rub her tummy. Our friend and his partner were amazed because she had never done this before even with them. So this was the icing on Jasper's cake because his mother had agreed with his decision.

HOME AT LAST

It was fun and games when we finally took him home. I learned how I was supposed to train a pup for it to grow it into a loving and obedient dog. Sadly for me Howard did not have or ever wanted to learn what I had learnt. He had his own book to work from but the only problem was he was writing the book as he went.

The first night I made a bed for Jasper (he told me this is what his name was) and we sort of settled down. The problem was Howard could not handle Jasper whimpering so he picked him up and put him on the bed. Well you know the rest and *yes* he never did leave the bed. A wonderful friendship was cemented taking us to some lows as well as some very high highs.

We fitted our life around Jasper as he chewed furniture, shoes, clothes all the usual things dogs do. He loved me but Howard was his best mate and so would do cart wheels for him, then expected Howard to reciprocate. I did take Jasper to puppy school but the one who was trained was me. Then when Jasper was ten months old Astral came into our lives.

ASTRAL'S ENTRY INTO OUR LIVES

A person who I knew in Queensland had a beautiful dog and a cat who decided it was time for her to have kittens. I was a very close to this person so when her cat had kittens I was nominated to be a forever mother to one of them. This was very confronting because the last thing I needed at the time was a kitten. We had Jasper who was well on the way to training us so why would we take on a kitten as well. I really did not need this kitten but for some reason I was not aware of, I agreed to take one.

I had to make arrangements for a cat cage for the kitten to travel from Queensland to Victoria in. Flight Arrangements were made for this tiny kitten. Everything was in place so all I had to do then was go to the freight terminal and pick up my precious cargo.

I arrived to pick up our kitten but was faced with a very perplexed attendant. They had a cage seemingly without an occupant. Due to them not being allowed to tamper with any cargo they had to wait until I arrived to open the door and check for a kitten. The person who sent me the kitten had put a tiny white pillow in the cage and when I moved it there was the most beautiful kitten I had laid eyes on.

I took him home and made him comfortable but Jasper was not quite as accommodating as I was. He lived with but did not totally accept this furry creature who walked in on his territory. I could not settle on a name for him until I hit on Astral because when looking at him he quite often seemed to be elsewhere. We all settled down into a routine of sorts.

Our next door neighbor had four rottweilers who were often bored and unhappy. We made sure there was nowhere along the fence line where our animals were in danger. We checked it out on more than one occasion and were satisfied that all was well. We had come to love our little friends totally and we knew it was incumbent on us to protect them.

JASPER AND ASTRAL FOREVER FRIENDS

One weekend when Astral was six months and Jasper sixteen months old we had cause to be away overnight. My youngest daughter said she would be home so would look after the animals. On the Sunday Howard had a very disturbing phone call from her. Instead of staying home that night she was invited to a party. Due to it being quite a distance from home she stayed there the night.

On arriving home she went looking for the animals. Then Astral came up to her so she picked him up then dropped him just quickly in fright. Where his right leg was supposed to be there was a large hole where her finger went into. She was extremely upset so rang Howard while sitting on the couch. With this Astral made his way into the lounge room then over to the couch so she picked him up and put him beside her. He put his paw on her to let her know he was okay and she was not to blame in any way whatsoever. Howard being the together one suggested she take him to a vet and have him looked at.

This she did and was fortunate enough to find a vet open not far from home. They took him in checked him out and were amazed to find him alive as a main artery had been torn but the wound was clean and intact. We were to learn Jasper had taken Astral under his paw to look after him until help arrived.

We returned home to realise Jasper was not just a dog hero was our hero. I had asked Jasper what had happened and with that he went outside and showed us where Astral had been playing. There was the tiniest gap where a plastic bag was sitting and it would seem Astral had been playing with the bag when one of the Rottweiler's decided to play with Astral, resulting in one leg missing.

Jasper then took us inside the house and showed us where he and Astral had travelled. They ended up behind a door in one of the bedrooms where there was a towel. We could see that Astral had certainly been on the towel and as it would seem Jasper had looked after him by continuously licking his wound while keeping him company. We also believed this happened on the Saturday and it was Sunday afternoon when Astral was found. From that day forward there was a bond cemented between this beautiful brave kitten and our little hero that would never be broken.

While Astral was at the vets they operated on his wound as well as taking away any chance he had of him fathering kittens. The vet who operated on Astral was amazed because not only had Astral's leg been taken but the whole shoulder was gone as well. He did say it was a miracle that Astral survived being so young and not getting immediate attention. Astral showed no signs of being traumatized, quite the opposite as we realised after talking to the vet staff.

When I picked Astral up from the vets the next day a member of the staff said they could not believe just how beautiful he was through the trauma. The person said on arrival Astral was purring then when he woke from his operation he was once again purring. Apparently many people had heard about this kitten in the short time he was at the vets. They were told just how wonderful and placid Astral was.

Astral adjusted well thanks to his now protector Jasper. At times Jasper was over protective but Astral took it in his stride because he knew his best mate had his best interests at heart. When we added Oscar the budgie to our clan (this is another story) Astral was not too happy so if Astral was not happy and neither was Jasper.

Astral would look at Oscar and cry then Jasper would do his utmost to try to help Astral get his nemesis in any way he possibly could. This game continued until one morning I noticed Oscar was not on his perch but was lying on the bottom of his cage. It was a sad day for me because Oscar helped me with my writing while making his bird noises to cheer me on to bigger and better things.

WORKING JASPER

Due to Jasper and Howard's relationship Jasper would go to work every day to meet his friends. His favorite would bring in delicious treats for himself and Jasper. Every morning Jasper would do a tour of the area around the factory and due to it being on an extremely busy intersection it was a dangerous thing to do. But Jasper being Jasper could not or would not be deterred from his morning constitutional. He would also venture to the railway station behind the factory and we knew this because many people informed us of his antics.

One day I was not at work so Howard had to do a delivery of parts to one of our customers with his mate Jasper. Unbeknown to Howard while he was unloading the parts Jasper decided to get out of the car and go for a stroll. Howard got back in the car and headed back to work when he received a phone call from the place he had just left. They asked him where his dog was and with that Howard realised Jasper was not with him so he turned the car around and headed back. On arrival he found Jasper nonchalantly waiting for him. The business owner told Howard that Jasper had seen him take off so chased after him for a short time then decided to go back and wait for his return. Jasper had never been to this factory before so it would seem once again his power of summing up a situation then taking action was unique. These people related this story to anyone who cared to listen.

Jasper loved being at work and many people loved to see him there. There was one couple who loved him so would travel a long distance on their motor bike of a Saturday morning just to see and play with him. He also had his critics and this was mainly due to the fact that Jasper didn't take to every person he met. He was an amazing judge of character and was always proven right until one man who had been a customer for many years thought Jasper was wonderful *but*. Howard never understood what "the *but*" was nonetheless Jasper never did make friends with this man. Then one day things went from bad to worse because this man brought his father with him and Jasper became friends with him very quickly but still would not accept the son.

Jasper was the workshop foreman who would check everything and everyone out to make sure things were running smoothly. We had a real crusty middle aged character working for us who didn't like or trust many people but for reasons unknown he took to Jasper. He knew of Jasper's exploits and his ability to judge a character. They had a few one on one meetings where they would exchange their ideas on people to always end up on the same page.

Then it came the time when Jasper wasn't so keen to come to work on a full time basis. The bed was more enticing than a day on the concrete floor, as well as the back seat of Howard's car. Many a time one of the workmen were told by Jasper to open the back door of Howard's car so he could jump inside and have his afternoon siesta. Everyone obliged because Jasper demanded. He loved to sit on Howard's knee while he ate his lunch and this continued to form the bond they had. Jasper knew when Howard needed him so he was always available.

The time came when Jasper would venture into work a couple of days a week. Every morning Howard and Jasper would share breakfast then when it was time for Howard to for leave work Jasper would either run to the front door or onto the bed to spend the day contemplating life. Jasper was not the type of dog who would run to greet us, he would take his time (I suppose you could say it was his grand entrance) and we would know if he was miffed at us for being away too long or happy to see us.

CON MAN JASPER

My eldest daughter was a cat not a dog person. Well Jasper picked this fact up very quickly and would challenge her at every turn. One day she was sitting on the couch and he jumped up beside her and kept moving closer and closer to her until she could not ignore him anymore. He was extremely defiant, he knew what he wanted so would leave no stone unturned until we saw things his way. No matter what, he was extremely protective of his family even the daughter who tried to ignore him. Eventually he got under her skin as he did so many people who came to love him.

A PUP?

During this time I brought another little Jack Russell (she had long legs and a fine body) into the fold and it would seem I was the only one happy with my decision. I went to our local Pets Paradise where there were a litter of pups waiting to be taken home with a trusted human. When the cage door was opened a female pup came up to me and said you are mine then proceeded to bite me on the nose. What was I supposed to do? The saddest part of this story was that Astral was not at all comfortable or happy with her being around. Make no mistake she was a handful so Astral went into hiding. It came to the stage we would arrive home at night to find he had disappeared.

The first time Astral disappeared we were beside ourselves with worry because we knew just how fearful he was since his run in with the Rottweiler. Howard was absolutely amazing, he found out where Astral was hiding which was under the vacant house next door (the Rottweiler house). Howard had to coerce and encourage Astral out for quite some time for many a night to come out. He then put him on a bench where Yasman (another story) could not reach him.

Howard worked with Astral for a long time before he was ready to cohabitate with Yasman. All this time Jasper was his protector and friend. Jasper tolerated Yasman barely and she kept trying to get his attention by biting and playing with his tail. Over time his tail went from thick and bushy to a very fine coating of wiry hair. Howard certainly lamented this fact on many occasions but what could I do?

Yasman ended up with the same fate as Jasper, sleeping on our bed. This was very tricky as Jasper loved to sleep beside Howard and Yasman would snuggle up under the bedding. This became our routine sleeping arrangement for now and in the future. Occasionally Astral decided he wanted a piece of the action so we made room for him as well.

MANICURIST?

There was also Jasper the manicurist. When he was young my youngest daughter would trim his nails for him. Initially Jasper was very content for her to do this until one day she took one of his nails too far down. He was not impressed at all so decided the only way to get the job done was to do it himself. This is exactly what he did; he chewed and pulled at his nails until he had the results he wanted. No human with clippers ever went near Jasper's nails again!

COMMANDO TRAINING?

There was also the time when I used to take both the dogs walking together. This brought me a lot of grief because trying to encourage two stubborn dogs to do the same thing at the same time was near impossible. It was now time to bring in a commando to help train the dogs. HA! What a joke. The commando I hired let me know in no uncertain terms it was myself and Howard who needed the training. I could see the smirk appear on Jasper's face as he was saying I told you so but you would not listen. When commando was around Jasper acted like a wonderfully trained dog whereas Yasman did not have the same acumen as Jasper so would just be herself.

By this time I had not told Howard what the commando had told me about us needing the training. When I did he said she did not know what she was talking about because Jasper was well trained and Yasman was still young.

I must admit I did learn a great deal from her but putting this learning into practice when she was not around was another thing altogether.

I know if Howard had put in a bit more effort we may have had a win. Eventually I came up with my very own brainwave and that was to take one dog at a time. Guess What? It worked! Too bad about the extra time it took me to achieve this but I didn't care because I worked with Howard and I had a perfect reason for turning up late.

OBEDIENT JASPER?

There was also Jasper the obedient. My youngest daughter loved Jasper but more importantly loved to tease him. He loved her dearly and so wanted to please her so she began to train him. It began with the usual shake hands and sit, then progressed. She then trained him to lay down, then there came time for him to roll over. Under sufferance Jasper eventually appeased her by rolling over. My daughter never wanted to show Jasper she was pleased with him although she would tell him he was clever. Jasper would look at her with the body language of, *what took you so long*.

Every time my daughter visited she and Jasper would go through the same routine. There were times he wasn't too impressed with her asking him to do his tricks. Eventually he would placate her then walk away with his head in the air. He would let her think she needed him more than he needed her. In actual fact he loved the games they played. Eventually he ended up with the ascendency because when she turned up he would proceed to do the tricks of his own volition. He would look at her with a smug look suggesting well there you go my job is over so let's have some fun.

Those two had a wonderful relationship especially after the drama with Astral. Jasper knew no matter what happened my daughter would always be there to help both he and Astral. Jasper definitely was not a vicious dog at all but he did not like people coming too close to him unless he gave them permission to do so. This was certainly the situation when my daughter had her son.

Jasper loved and protected him with his life if necessary. My grandson could do anything to Jasper and he would never blink an eye as was his love for him. As my grandson got older their relationship strengthened and they learnt a great deal from each other. Admittedly my grandson had a pet name for Jasper and that was grumbles because he seemed to grumble about everything and anything.

As I am writing this story Astral has come into the office and is harassing me. He is trying to get up on my knee which is an impossibility. He keeps talking and nagging me so eventually I get a nice warm blanket put it on the floor for him to lie on. He has appeased me by doing this and is so content that he has gone to sleep (no surprise where a cat is concerned). This certainly is not a usual thing for him to do as he would rather be in front of the heater. It is obvious to me he is tuned into his old friend Jasper and wants to be a part of my writing his and Jasper's story.

YOGA ASTRAL

Astral surprised me one day when I was doing yoga. I love yoga because it is so peaceful and consumes my whole being. Astral must have thought it was pretty good because one day he wanted to be a part of the action. He was enjoying himself while I was trying to maneuver myself around him particularly when I was doing the balancing poses.

He decided it looked like fun so he proceeded to head butt me while purring. This may have been fun for him but it was not so for me although I always find myself smiling whenever I think of his antics. Until this day he still joins me in doing my yoga, sometimes he is a participant and others he watches from the sidelines (comfortable chair with fluffy blanket) to give me his encouragement.

GAINING CONFIDENCE

Whenever anyone would turn up at our home Astral would hide. He was very fearful of people who were not a part of his life before he lost his leg. Quite often he would venture outside and hide under the house or in one of the inside cupboards. It was not just a cat not wanting to be seen, it was a cat in fear. Initially he kept away from my grandson but this didn't deter my grandson as he would always talk to Astral because he loved him. He persevered until one night when he was staying with us Astral eventually allowed my grandson to pat him. Since then Astral has allowed our other grandchildren to pat and love him as well.

JASPER THE PEACE MAKER

There were times when we would have fish or chicken and Astral would make a fuss to have some. Jasper would then take control by lecturing Astral and if that did not work he would get on top of him and hold him down. This also happened when Howard would have either ice cream in a bowl or on a stick. It ended with Howard giving Astral a lick or two followed by Yasman and then Jasper would finish the rest off. It's not the big things in life that create best memories; it's all the little everyday things.

This is where wonderful and lasting memories are created to cheer us up when we are feeling down. All you need are memories of all the precious moments you carry within to cheer you up. Animals are reflectors of humans so if you treat them badly that's what they reflect, conversely if you treat them with love and respect that's exactly what you will receive in return.

PACIFYER JASPER

Quite a few years ago I decided to open a shop in Marysville. I had been looking for a shop closer to home but nothing felt right. I opened my shop and after I had been there for a while Howard had to go away for a few days. I was to look after the animals so Howard put cat in cage and dog on the back seat, then set off for Marysville.

Naturally I was not in the car but I did have exactly the same experience when I brought cat and dog for a holiday previously. Astral would start to meow then cry. Jasper was not too happy because he enjoyed a ride in the car so he would tell Astral off in a very low and guttural voice that Astral understood. He would settle down for a while then would begin to carry on again so once again Jasper would tell him off in no uncertain terms until he stopped. It was really amazing to hear because Jasper's way of communicating was definitely unique to him.

UNSOCIABLE JASPER

There was a Sunday when Jasper, Astral and Howard came to visit me in Marysville. As I was working Howard and Jasper came to visit me in the shop. There were numerous people around so Jasper obviously found himself bored with the whole situation. I knew this because I received a phone call from a friend who said *I just saw your dog walking up the hill towards your house.*

We checked to see if Jasper was around and sure enough he was nowhere to be found. So up to the house Howard went and sure enough there was Jasper. He had had enough so off home he went. Jasper certainly had a mind of his own and would use it when required. He was a wonderful example of living in the moment. If something is not working this moment then wait because there is another one, then another and so on.

FEARFUL JASPER

Jasper never got caught up in anything apart from thunder storms and fireworks. I know many dogs suffer badly from these, but when it's your dog you love it's very hard to watch them go through the pain they experience from nature and man. Nature you can understand and deal with but fireworks to please humans is another thing altogether.

A momentary pleasure for humans can take an animal on a journey through pain and fear. Where or when does the human ego ever acknowledge anything other than itself? It doesn't because all you have to do is hear of the number of dogs who run away from their home due to the pain humans have caused in the name of fun. Humans say they had a wonderful time watching all the colors lighting up the night sky with families revelling in the event, but how long does it last? What, until the next day, the next week because they may forget but the dog certainly does not!

JASPER AND VETS

I'm sure I am a good dog and cat owner because I made sure they kept up with their vaccinations and any problems that surfaced from time to time would end in a visit to the vets. Jasper was a problem for me. Every time the vet staff saw me sitting in the waiting room with Jasper at my feet on his lead they cringed. The problems would begin when he had to be weighed.

Anything was preferable to getting on that thing and standing still when I knew he wanted to be anywhere other than where he was. He would then sit and size up all the other animals in the room (whether this was a reflection of me I would prefer to say negative but sadly it must have been positive) until he was called into *the room*.

The vet would look at the piece of paper in his hand at Jasper's past performances in aghast. I would be asked to put him on the table (this is where my fitness level needed to be at its optimum). He was a small to medium dog but this was no help to me at all. At home I could lift him without a problem but here, no way. He would growl, snap and complain until the vet diagnosed him as a vicious dog who needed a muzzle. This was our routine whenever I took him to visit the vet. Jasper muzzled, me harassed and very apologetic. My dog is not like this, he is even tempered, would not hurt anyone -*yeah right*- said the vet. This scenario never improved whenever we went to visit the vet.

I kept saying to Howard that Jasper was more his dog than mine so he should do some of these bonding things with him. Eventually he did! And guess what? He obviously had another Jasper because this one was absolutely perfect-never put a paw wrong. He did everything asked of him without so much as a whimper. This vet was amazed after reading his history and then the persona Jasper presented to him.

Howard would come home and say, *"I don't know what all the fuss is about because he did everything he was supposed to, muzzle free."* Obviously the problem had to be me as it was same dog, same vet practice, the only difference was it was Howard rather than me taking him. After that I decided it was Howard's job to take him to the vet when required and I never let go of my white surrender flag.

BEACH BOY JASPER

When our business moved from one premises to another we found ourselves next to a doggy day care centre. This proved to be a very good move because we enrolled Jasper to attend for two days a week. They did wonderful dog things like going for walks, playing games and if you were really good you got plenty of attention (Jasper believed cuddles were not for him so attention would suffice).

Jasper initially seemed to enjoy the whole adventure but eventually he was bored and lost interest. He would let us know in no uncertain terms as to his feelings so this was the end of his day care days until summer came around.

The woman who ran the business let us know they would be having a beach day every alternate Friday and would Jasper like to attend. There was no doubt what Jasper's answer would be as he loved water. Friday would come around and Jasper was the pup again. The dogs would be bused to the beach and then let loose to play, and play they certainly did.

Out of all the dogs there Jasper was the best, he had more fun than the others and his energy level was very high. They named him the beach dog and we have some photos to prove it. Whenever Jasper saw water his eyes would light up and he would swim, then swim some more until he had nothing more to give. We had many fulfilling and enjoyable hours watching Jasper in water.

SENSITIVE JASPER

There was a time when my grandson was staying with us. One morning Jasper, Yasman my grandson and I went for our morning walk. Everything was in order until Jasper went to the side of the road and stood in his protective stance. With that I went over to look at what he was protecting and there I found a Blue Tongue Lizard who seemed to have been broken.

I say this because it could not move and there was a tiny little baby lizard standing up trying to protect its mother. I have never experienced anything like it as this baby was spitting at anyone who went near its mother. Jasper was amazing with the concern he showed these two. I went home and found a box and a towel to wrap the mother in with her baby beside her then took them to the wild life rescue house in our area.

My grandson was intrigued with the number of baby kangaroos in the wild life rescue house. He was able to pat one and this certainly brought a very large smile to his face. When the woman looked at the lizard she said it was in a great deal of pain as its back had been broken so she gently put it to sleep. The baby was certainly a feisty little creature who was put in a place of its own to grow into a beautiful adult like its mother. The baby owed its life to Jasper because if he had walked on rather than stop, there would have been a very different ending for both the mother and baby.

JASPER'S TIME

Life went on sort of smoothly until Jasper turned thirteen. We believed we would have him for many years to come but he had other ideas. At times when I looked at him I somehow knew he would not be with us for much longer. I even mentioned this to Howard once but realistically I didn't want to say too much. Health wise he had the exact same problems as Howard. He had an enlarged heart and problems with his lungs affecting his breathing. We began to notice he was having trouble jumping up on his beloved bed. He was a bit crankier than usual but apart from that he seemed to be okay.

Then one night in May 2012 Jasper became sick and could not keep his food down. So the next day I made a vet appointment for Jasper and a doctor's appointment for Howard. (Both with the same problem.) Howard double checked with me that I had the bookings right, Howard doctor and Jasper vet. Howard had the next day off work and took Jasper to the vet then they spent a lovely day together.

The next morning while getting ready to go to work I was frustrated because I wanted to sit on the couch with Jasper to eat my breakfast and time was running out. Then something amazing happened. I sat down with Jasper and time seemed to slow down so I was able to spend more precious time with him as I knew his health was deteriorating. The vet had prescribed medication and was not too concerned with his condition. When leaving for work Howard said his usual goodbye to his great mate.

That night the 9th May 2012 Jasper was not around when we arrived home from work. We knew he was not inside the house where he would usually be. Howard then picked up his torch and went looking outside. Due to the bond Jasper and Howard had, Howard knew where he would be and sure enough there he was lying under a tree facing the lake we love.

His beautiful spirit had crossed over to the rainbow bridge waiting for us to join him. He waited until we were nearly home before his spirit passed over because his beautiful body was still warm. Howard then wrapped him in one of his shirts and dug a grave and buried him where he found his body. The remarkable part of this was that Jasper was never a real outside dog. He would come if we were outside but as for sitting under that tree, well he never did. When Howard was burying Jasper Astral turned up and let out an almighty howl and then cried as friends do for friends and more importantly for Jasper his protector.

Only people who have loved an animal can know what we went through that night. There are no adequate words to describe the surfacing emotions. A couple of weeks prior to this I was in bed reading and as Howard was walking into the bathroom he stopped at the bedroom door. There was a commotion at the window behind my head. Howard was amazed at what he was witnessing.

He told me there was an owl standing on a very narrow window ledge looking straight at him. I then turned around and saw this magnificent creature of the night and indeed it was looking at Howard. Somewhere within me I knew but I didn't want to know. It was such an amazing experience but knowing they are messengers of death there could only be one reason. We have never seen an owl before or since that one time. He was conveying to Howard that Jasper his best friend would be well looked after and of this we have no doubt.

JASPER MY PROTECTOR

Jasper was my protector when Howard was not home. I was confronted by my demons and Jasper would always be near to protect me. If needed he would have given his life for me because he knew just how much Howard loved me and wanted me to be safe. My life was so much richer for having Jasper as a huge part of it. I love dogs and I love nothing more than seeing human – dog relationships. The love that passes between human and dog brings with it loyalty, protection, humility- and huge doses of *Unconditional Love*. A dog will listen to our problems and inner fears then will lick you to say I understand and *I love you*.

Jasper was more than a dog and there are many people who knew and loved him who would say the same. He had his needs and he demanded them be met, *HIS WAY*!

Astral is still with us and is an extremely contented and at times demanding cat. At this very moment he is scratching on the door frame to be let in. He and Yasman have made a truce and in true female style she is very protective of him. I am sure Jasper has given her a lecture or two on the pros and cons of looking after Astral.

After Jasper passed over he gave me this story for Howard

A TRIBUTE TO MY BEST MATE HOWARD

I was born on the 12ᵗʰ January 1999. By this time you were still trying to get your head around the fact you and me were going to be great mates. HA! I knew this but you did not.

You didn't know how you could possibly make room in your life for a dog. There were so many questions and so much uncertainty on your part. I had no fears because I chose you. I knew you were special. I knew the relationship was not a human – dog show. This partnership was based on *love respect loyalty friendship* and *responsibility* to and for each other.

I knew you before you knew me but I certainly opened your heart wide and deep when I was a few days old and you turned up to check me out. Even with my eyes not yet open I crawled over to you and laid on your shoe. Our physical connection was made and we both knew a love so strong was born, never ever to be challenged or swayed in any way whatsoever.

I was at peace because our life together had begun.

I knew you were a soft touch when you took me home with you and allowed me to take charge. Bernadette would say no maybe; you would say yes definitely. I was never going to sleep anywhere other than right beside you and this we did. I loved every moment we spent together. You shared every part of yourself with me. By doing this I gave you everything I had because you would never neglect or hurt me. You accepted my fears with your compassion and your love. Even though at the time I was so scared I appreciated your caring. I never got used to the thunder, lightning or really loud noises but knowing you were there helped so much.

I used to love going to work with you but as time marched on I found the bed more appealing than the car seat and concrete floor.

I respected you and I know you respected me after I helped Astral to live. I never really cared overly much for Astral until he was mauled by that huge dog next door. I knew I had to do everything within my power to save him and I did. I knew what you would have done so I couldn't let you down.

We went through everything together. We understood each other as no one else could. I felt your pain, your loneliness, your sense of responsibility and most of all your *unconditional love*. I let you know in every way I could that my time with you would be completed sooner rather than later. I gave you everything of myself so I left you in the physical world on my terms – when I was ready.

I knew you would understand why I chose the place I did to leave my body. I know how much you love your lake and your property, so this was my last gift to you. I know I had your blessing, but it was never going to be easy.

My body is now melding with the land but my spirit and my love for you is never ending.

We are still together, you just cannot see me. I appreciate the conversations we still have and when it is time for you to leave your body, I will be waiting for you at the rainbow bridge so we can cross over together.

Your best mate
Jasper

Nothing can equal the love and devotion a dog and cat can give and there are many animal lovers around the world who know.

TO ALL THE ANIMAL LOVERS IN THIS WORLD ALL I CAN SAY IS A BIG

THANK YOU!

AFTERWORD

I have been writing my stories for a number of years thinking I was learning about myself. I believed I was making headway until I re-read these stories where a wakeup call was awaiting me.

Many occasions I would pick up a story then read it only to realise I had very little idea of what I was talking about. I had no idea of where my head was at because it all seemed foreign to me. Sometimes I would read a story then update it and then pick it up some time later to update it once again.

I have had to challenge myself to know who the real sustainable me is. There were many and varied books I read but unless I was prepared to put actions into words nothing was going to change. At times I believed I could jump a few steps but I came to realise that was never going to happen.

There was also a time in my life when I believed I was well on my way to knowing *it all* to *get there*. I now realise I must have been an amazing person then because now I read books and watch DVDs as well as listen to cds and still have so much to learn. I shake my head at my arrogance because my then attitude took me absolutely nowhere.

I found it convenient to cocoon myself in a group of like minded people. I would hang onto every word someone who I thought was really there uttered while in reality I was holding myself prisoner in myself created jail. But, if I had not had these experiences I would not be writing the book you now have in your possession.

I have learned there are no shortcuts or fast tracking because unless we experience for ourselves we will *never know*. There are no winners or losers, prizes or penalties as we are all equal, we just have to know it.

On mine and Yasman's walk this morning I knew the totality of being a part of all there is. I was the tree and the gravel as well as the sky and the magpies who were serenading everyone who wanted to hear.

I thank God every day for every blessing in my life. I have learnt not to look for something big to come into my life because every moment holds more than I could ever have imagined. There is one mantra that kept me in the here and now when I was anywhere but here in the now. It is simple but it brought many miracles into my life.

LET GO, LET GOD

Thank you God and thank you every person who has read this book and I wish you all well in knowing who you are. Nothing belongs to or comes from anyone other than yourself, so take responsibility for you and your life.

I wish you all the very best and thank you

Yours truly
Bernadette Reynolds